C000135853

"The Production of a Female Pen"

Artist Unknown. *Elizabeth Duchess Dowager of Kingston*
taken at the Bar of the House of Lords.
Etching. 17.5 x 10 cm, sheet.
Published by G. Robinson
1 May 1776.

"The Production of a Female Pen":
Anna Larpent's Account of the
Duchess of Kingston's Bigamy Trial of 1776

A FACSIMILE EDITION

Transcribed and with an introduction by
Matthew J. Kinservik

saevis Liburnis scilicet invidens
privata deduci superbo
non humilis mulier triumpho.
　　　　—Horace *Carmina* I.xxxvii

Published by
The Lewis Walpole Library · Yale University
Miscellaneous Antiquities, Number XVII

Distributed by
University Press of New England

Copyright © 2004 Yale University

Library of Congress Cataloging-in-Publication Data

Larpent, Anna Margaretta, 1758–1832.
  The production of a female pen : Anna Larpent's account
of the Duchess of Kingston's bigamy trial of 1776 / transcribed
and with an introduction by Matthew J. Kinservik.— Facsimile ed.
      p. cm. — (Miscellaneous antiquities ; no. 17)
  Based on a manuscript at the Lewis Walpole Library, Yale University.
  ISBN 0-8457-3154-8 (alk. paper)
    1. Bristol, Elizabeth Chudleigh, Countess of, 1720–1788—Trials,
litigation, etc. 2. Trials (Bigamy)—England.   I. Kinservik,
Matthew J., 1967–   II. Lewis Walpole Library, Yale University.   III. Title.   IV. Series.
  KD372.C58L37 2004
  345.42'0283—dc22
                                                    2004010588

PRINTED IN THE UNITED STATES OF AMERICA

Contents

Preface

In 1772 Horace Walpole published two issues of *Miscellaneous Antiquities*, both in editions of 525 copies. He intended to satisfy what he gauged to be a general "taste for anecdotes and historic papers, for ancient letters that record affairs of state, illustrate characters of remarkable persons, or preserve the memory of former manners and customs." Walpole's admirable plan was to publish entertaining original manuscripts and printed pieces, "now little known," from his own and his friends' collections. He over-estimated the public's capacity for such amusements, however, as he wrote to his friend Mason in March 1773: "The *Miscellaneous Antiquities* have not sold above a fifth of them, so there will be no more."

In 1927, as he recalls in *Collector's Progress*, W. S. Lewis had the temerity to resume Walpole's short-lived series. He was confident that the present taste was "identical with that of 1772" and would embrace antiquities of the sort to be found in his library. As it happened, the first three numbers of Lewis's *Miscellaneous Antiquities* resulted in almost the same disappointing sales as did Walpole's: from editions of 500 copies, only about 130 were sold. Lewis's response was not to abandon the project entirely but to carry on with the series until 1940, privately printing what he calls "odds and ends" from his collection in small editions as Christmas keepsakes.

Given this history, it may appear foolhardy to launch a second revival of *Miscellaneous Antiquities*. Nevertheless, the presence in The Lewis Walpole Library's collections of materials that are unknown, or known only to a few scholars, has encouraged the present Editor to resume the series. Scholarly approaches to the eighteenth century have shifted since Lewis set out to build on Walpole's project, to be sure, but the value to scholarship of primary sources is if anything clearer now than it was in the 1920s. It is, then, with great pleasure that the Editor announces the Library's revival of this venerable series with the publication of Anna Porter Larpent's manuscripts describing the 1776 trial of the Duchess of Kingston for bigamy.

MARGARET K. POWELL
The Lewis Walpole Library

ACKNOWLEDGMENTS

The research for this monograph was made possible by a fellowship, awarded jointly by the American Society for Eighteenth Century Studies and The Lewis Walpole Library, for a month of study at The Lewis Walpole Library in July 2001. I am particularly grateful to Margaret Powell, Anna Malicka, and Joan Sussler for their help, and to David Turner, Romita Ray, John Beynon, and Heather McPherson for their friendship and suggestions during our time in residence at the Library. Thanks also to Robert Hume, Judith Milhous, Ruth Yeazell, Paul Cannan, David Turner, and Jonathan Grossman, who all offered helpful suggestions on the draft of the introduction. For their suggestions and encouragement I am also grateful to Joseph Roach and all of the participants at the anti-theatricality conference held at The Lewis Walpole Library in March 2002. Finally, I owe a great debt to James Mooney for his careful proofreading and his advice on the transcription of the manuscripts.

ADVERTISEMENT,

BY THE EDITORS.

THE taſte for anecdotes and hiſtoric papers, for ancient letters that record affairs of ſtate, illuſtrate characters of remarkable perſons, or preſerve the memory of former manners and cuſtoms, was never more general than at preſent. To indulge this diſpoſition in the public and in themſelves, the Editors of the following pages, being poſſeſſed of ſeveral original MSS. and being promiſed the uſe of others, propoſe to publiſh in numbers ſome of the moſt entertaining: at the ſame time intending to mix with them other pieces formerly printed, now little known, and not to be met with but by accident. Nor will the numbers appear with any periodic regularity, but as it ſhall ſuit the leiſure and convenience of the Gentlemen who have undertaken

the

the work, which is in imitation of Peck's Deſiderata Curioſa, and is ſolely calculated for amuſement; for which reaſon the Editors make no promiſes, enter into no engagements; but ſhall take the liberty of continuing, varying, or dropping the plan, when and in what manner they pleaſe---a notice they think right to give, that no man may complain hereafter of being diſappointed.

Advertisement from *Miscellaneous Antiquities* of 1772.

The above was written for the first number of the *Miscellaneous Antiquities* by Horace Walpole in 1772. The present taste being so identical with that of 1772, it is with great pleasure that the modern Editors announce the resumption of this work, which they trust will not fail to please when it follows so polite and elegant a model.

Advertisement from *Miscellaneous Antiquities* 3, the first number in W. S. Lewis's revival of Walpole's series, of 1927.

MISCELLANEOUS
ANTIQUITIES;

OR,

A COLLECTION OF

CURIOUS PAPERS:

Either republifhed from SCARCE TRACTS, or now
firft printed from ORIGINAL MSS.

NUMBER I.

TO BE CONTINUED OCCASIONALLY.

Invenies illic et fefta domeftica vobis.
Sæpe tibi Pater eft, fæpe legendus Avus.

OVID. Faft. lib. I.

STRAWBERRY-HILL:

PRINTED BY THOMAS KIRGATE, M.DCC.LXXII.

Title page from the first number of Horace Walpole's *Miscellaneous Antiquities.*

Miscellaneous Antiquities

*The first two numbers were edited
by Horace Walpole, the remainder
by W. S. Lewis, excepting as noted.*

1. *Honour Military and Civill.* Strawberry Hill, 1772. (525)
2. *The Life of Sir Thomas Wyatt, The Elder.* Strawberry Hill, 1772. (525)
3. *A Note Book of Horace Walpole.* New York: William Edwin Rudge, 1927. (500)
4. *Notes by Lady Louisa Stuart on George Selwyn and His Contemporaries, by John Heneage Jesse.* Edited from the Original Manuscript by W. S. Lewis. New York: Oxford University Press; London: H. Milford, 1928. (500)
5. *Horace Walpole's Fugitive Verses.* Edited by W. S. Lewis. New York: Oxford University Press; London: H. Milford, 1931. (500)
6. *The Forlorn Printer: Being Notes on Horace Walpole's Alleged Neglect of Thomas Kirgate*, by W. S. Lewis. Walpole Printing Office, 1931. (50)
7. *Anecdotes told me by Lady Denbigh*, [by] Horace Walpole. Farmington, Conn.: Priv. print., 1932. (50)
8. *Horace Walpole's Letter from Madame de Sévigné*, by W. S. Lewis. Farmington, Conn.: Priv. print., 1933. (100)
9. *Some Short Observations for the Lady Mary Stanhope Concerning The Writing of Ordinary Letters, By Philip, second Earl of Chesterfield.* Edited by W. S. Lewis. Farmington, Conn.: Priv. print., 1934. (100)
10. *Le Triomphe de l'Amitié, ou, l'Histoire de Jacqueline et de Jeanneton*, by W. S. Lewis. Farmington, Conn.: Priv. print., 1935. (100)
11. *The Duchess of Portland's Museum*, by Horace Walpole; with an introduction by W. S. Lewis. New York: The Grolier Club, 1936. (450)
12. *Bentley's Designs for Walpole's Fugitive Pieces*, by W. S. Lewis. Farmington, Conn.: Priv. print., 1936. (100)
13. *Memoranda Walpoliana*, with an introduction by W. S. Lewis. Farmington, Conn.: Priv. print., 1937. (100)
14. *Letters to and from Madame du Deffand and Julie de Lespinasse.* Edited by Warren Hunting Smith. New Haven: Yale University Press, 1938. (500)
15. *The Impenetrable Secret, probably Invented by Horace Walpole.* An Explanation of the Secret. With a Note on the Original by W. S. Lewis. Farmington, Conn.: Priv. print., 1939. (100)
16. *Notes by Horace Walpole on Several Characters of Shakespeare.* Edited by W. S. Lewis, Farmington, Conn.: Priv. print., 1940.

"The whole world is occupied
with the Duchess of Kingston's trial"

HORACE WALPOLE TO WILLIAM COLE
16 April 1776[1]

On 15 April 1776, the House of Lords convened as a jury in Westminster Hall to try the Duchess of Kingston for bigamy. During the five-day trial, the hall was transformed into a theatre-in-the-round that featured bleacher seating, galleries, and private boxes surrounding a large open area where the lords heard the duchess's case. Among the four thousand spectators was Anna Margaretta Larpent. Her voluminous journals, written later in life, record her attendance in only the sparest terms, and scholars who have studied Larpent's diaries lament the fact that her early papers (including those from 1776) are presumably lost.[2] But in the manuscript collection of The Lewis Walpole Library, catalogued under Anna Porter, Larpent's maiden name, are thirty-eight manuscript pages that record in great detail her observations on the Duchess of Kingston's trial. It is the earliest known manuscript by Anna Larpent and so it adds considerably to our understanding of her life and conflicted attitudes toward women's writing. It also greatly enhances our understanding of the Duchess of Kingston's trial.

A diplomat's daughter, Anna was one of the lucky people who had managed to get tickets to each day of the trial.[3] On the first day, she was fortunate enough to join Lady Bathurst and thirty-four others in the Lord High Steward's box. As Lord High Steward, Henry Bathurst was the presiding official at the trial, so to sit in his box was to occupy one of the best seats in the house. From this vantage point, Anna witnessed the beginning of one of the most scandalous trials of the age of George III.

1 *The Correspondence of Horace Walpole*, vol. 2, *Letters to the Reverend William Cole*, ed. W. S. Lewis and A. Dayle Wallace (New Haven: Yale University Press, 1938), 10.

2 See John Brewer, "Reconstructing the Reader: Prescriptions, Texts, and Strategies in Anna Larpent's Reading," in *The Practice and Representation of Reading in England*, ed. James Raven, Helen Small, and Naomi Tadmor (Cambridge: Cambridge University Press, 1996), 226-45; John Brewer, *The Pleasures of the Imagination: English Culture in the Eighteenth Century*

(Chicago: University of Chicago Press, 1997), ch. 2; and Claire Miller Colombo, "'This Pen of Mine Will Say Too Much': Public Performance in the Journals of Anna Larpent," *Texas Studies in Language and Literature* 38 (1996): 285-301.

3 To avoid the confusion of alternating "Larpent" and "Porter," I will hereafter refer simply to "Anna." Similarly, to avoid alternating between "Elizabeth Chudleigh," "Elizabeth Hervey," "Elizabeth Pierrepont," "Duchess of Kingston," and "Countess of Bristol," I will generally refer to "Elizabeth."

Although four thousand spectators fit into the hall, the demand for seats far out-paced the supply, and tickets for this spectacle were scarcer than tickets for David Garrick's farewell performances at Drury Lane that spring. (At twenty guineas each, they were significantly more expensive.) Hoping to capitalize on the enormous interest in the trial, one enterprising bookseller hastily reissued an account of the 1706 bigamy trial of Robert Fielding, offering it as a consolation prize to those who did not gain entry to the hall. Attached to it, and also sold separately, is a print with a view of the interior of Westminster Hall along with a key, indicating where the famous people sat.[4]

There are some valuable contemporary accounts of the trial from practiced gossips like Horace Walpole and Hannah More, but Anna's account is of special interest. First, it is a hitherto unknown and very lengthy account, running to thirty-eight pages of manuscript, full of unusual details and shrewd personal observations. The manuscript is, in fact, two documents: one is a six-page letter to a friend, written "to the moment" in Richardsonian style. The other is a more formal account, written after the fact for the enjoyment of a group of female friends who did not have tickets. In these documents, Anna ranges from seemingly superficial topics such as the duchess's dress and the sex appeal of the lawyers to lucid summaries of the major points at law to a deeply emotional response to the duchess's predicament. There is no comparable account of this important trial in print or manuscript.

The second reason Anna's observations are of special interest is because she is better known as Anna Larpent, wife of John Larpent, whom she married in 1782. He was Examiner of Plays, chief censor of the London stage from 1778 until his death in 1824. Anna is known to have assisted him in his censorial duties, sometimes censoring texts on her own. She was also a prolific diarist: her journals for the years 1773-1830 fill seventeen volumes. Recently, she has become a subject of study as an important Romantic Era woman for her work as both a censor and a diarist.[5] Because Anna expurgated her early journals later in life when she included them in her "Method-ized Journal," we have the opportunity to compare how she responded to the duchess's trial as an unmarried eighteen-year-old to how she thought fit to record it as an older, married woman.

But what makes The Lewis Walpole Library manuscripts most compelling is that

4 Advertisement in the *Public Ledger*, 16 April 1776.
5 See note 2 above and L. W. Conolly, "The Censor's Wife at the Theater: The Diary of Anna Margaretta Larpent, 1790-1800," *Huntington Library Quarterly* 35 (1971): 49-64; Jeffrey N. Cox, "Baillie, Siddons, Lar-pent: Gender, Power, and Politics in the Theatre of Romanticism," in *Women in British Romantic Theatre: Drama, Performance, and Society, 1790-1840*, ed. Catherine Burroughs (Cambridge: Cambridge University Press, 2000), 23-43.

they show us how a conservative and pious woman of the late eighteenth century regarded one of the most notorious women of the era. Anna's moral rectitude and sense of feminine propriety were very orthodox for her time, and while she was intelligent, shrewd, and opinionated, she was careful not to display these qualities too openly. The Duchess of Kingston, by contrast, was notoriously unconventional and flamboyant all her life, even during her trial. Despite the profound differences between the two, Anna does not simply denounce the duchess, as Lady Mary Coke and Horace Walpole do. Instead, while critical of the duchess, Anna is also surprisingly sympathetic to her at times. Similarly, Anna criticizes the sensational nature of the trial, but is eager to participate in the spectacle. She feels compelled to discuss many aspects of the event, but is mindful that her gender limits her freedom as a commentator. Accordingly, this pair of important manuscripts considerably enhances our conception of Anna while providing a fascinating commentary on one of the most sensational trials of the late eighteenth century.

I. The Duchess of Kingston's Bigamy

In order to make sense of these manuscripts, we need first to understand the complex and improbable string of events that led to the trial. The marital history of Elizabeth Chudleigh, "calling herself Duchess Dowager of Kingston" (as the legal formula put it), is a case study in the arcane marriage laws of the eighteenth century. It began near midnight in a clandestine ceremony in a country chapel in Lainston, near Winchester. On 4 August 1744, under cover of darkness, Elizabeth secretly married Augustus Hervey, a naval lieutenant and second son of the famous Lord Hervey and Mary (Molly) Lepell. The ceremony was conducted by the neighboring vicar and was attended by Elizabeth's aunt, a cousin, a family friend, and a servant named Anne Craddock, the last of whom supplied damning testimony against Elizabeth in her bigamy trial. The church was lit by a single taper stuck in the brim of one of the men's hat. There was no license, no publication of the banns, and no parish clerk to register the wedding—indeed, there was no church, just a little-used family chapel. Yet it was a perfectly legal and binding marriage.

Before the reforms of Lord Hardwicke's Marriage Act of 1753, there were many ways to get married in England, with or without a church ceremony. Unlike the continental nations, both Protestant and Catholic, that reformed their marriage laws after the Council of Trent in 1563, England retained vestiges of medieval marriage practice well into the eighteenth century. That situation made regulation and verification of marriages exceedingly difficult for the Church of England and the civil authorities. The Church of England encouraged a public ceremony performed by a minister before a congregation between the canonical hours of eight o'clock and noon. The ceremony was to be preceded by the public reading of the banns on three consecutive Sundays before the ceremony or by authority of a license from the church. But despite these guidelines and a number of attempts at reform by Parliament (as well as the interruption of the interregnum, when a system of civil marriage was instituted), the old, loose marriage system survived in England until 1753.[6]

Although a simple exchange of present-tense vows, or "spousals," was enough to establish marriage, a long campaign by the church courts against such unions resulted in a steady decline of their use over the seventeenth century.[7] By the eighteenth century, the Church of England was largely successful in establishing the importance of some sort of church involvement in the marriage compact. As a consequence, while clandestine marriage could take many forms, those who chose to avoid a public ceremony and the publication of the banns increasingly opted, like Elizabeth and Augustus Hervey, for a clandestine ceremony that offered the sanctity of a minister reading the marriage rite from the Book of Common Prayer.[8] The secrecy afforded by clandestine marriages was popular for a number of reasons. Some wished to avoid publication of the banns because they either had married or promised to marry another person and could be exposed. Others wished to avoid being teased by their friends and neighbors for getting married. This desire for privacy was especially prevalent among the social elites during the long eighteenth century, an attitude that Fanny Burney shared as late as 1768 when she remarked, "I don't suppose any thing can be so dreadful as a publick Wedding."[9] Still others, like Elizabeth and Augustus Hervey, wished to marry without the knowledge of their parents.

Hervey's reason for keeping the marriage a secret from his family is more obvious than Elizabeth's. His family was a famous and noble one; Elizabeth would not have been an advantageous match in the eyes of his relatives. Her father, lieutenant-governor of the Chelsea Hospital, had died when she was a girl, leaving Elizabeth and her mother with little. Under the patronage of William Pulteney, Elizabeth became

6 Lawrence Stone, *Road to Divorce: England 1630-1987* (Oxford: Oxford University Press, 1990), ch. 2.

7 Martin Ingram, *Church Courts, Sex and Marriage in England, 1570-1640* (Cambridge: Cambridge University Press, 1987), 209. For an explanation of spousal law and other forms of marriage formation, see 189-218.

8 For a discussion of types of clandestinity, see R. B. Outhwaite, *Clandestine Marriage in England, 1500-1850* (London: Hambledon Press, 1995), 19-49.

9 *The Early Journals and Letters of Fanny Burney*, vol. 1, *1768-1773*, ed. Lars E. Troide (Oxford: Clarendon Press, 1988), 18. For a discussion of the trend toward privacy, see Jeremy Boulton, "Itching after Private Marryings: Marriage Customs in Seventeenth-Century London," *London Journal* 16 (1991): 15-34.

IPHIGENIA.

Price.

Artist Unknown. *Iphigenia*. Etching & engraving. 35 x 22 cm, sheet.
In *The Trial of the Duchess of Kingston for Bigamy*. London: House of Peers, 1776, facing page 14. 749.5.1.1.

a Maid of Honor to Augusta, Princess of Wales, in 1743, a position that provided her not just an introduction to London society and the Leicester House group, but also a much needed salary of £200 a year. If she married, she would become ineligible for her post and would lose the salary that supported her and her mother, so she married clandestinely and kept the union a secret. Why she went behind her mother's back is unclear. Indeed, why she married Hervey at all is a mystery. The two barely knew each other; she was said to have been in love with the Duke of Hamilton; and Hervey was shipped out on duty just days after the marriage. It was a union they both came to regret and devoutly wished to be extricated from.

While Hervey was at sea during most of the late 1740s, Elizabeth gained prominence as one of the beauties of the Leicester House court. She is rumored to have caught the eye and fancy of George II at the Jubilee Ball in 1749, where she arrested the attention of all London because of her notoriously sheer costume. Held at Ranelagh, the masquerade was a royal event in honor of the Peace of Aix-la-Chapelle. Elizabeth appeared as Iphigenia in a gown so sheer that her breasts were plainly visible. Before entering the garden, she is reputed to have said that she was, like Iphigenia, "ready for the sacrifice!" Lady Elizabeth Montague said that she was so naked "that the high priest could very easily inspect the entrails of the victim."[10] Several suggestive prints celebrate her audacious costume, and Iphigenia was a nickname that stuck to her for the rest of her life.

Elizabeth moved in powerful circles, but as her conduct at the Jubilee Ball shows, she was more notorious than respectable. She ran up huge debts at London gaming tables, which Hervey was obligated to pay. In his journal from these years, he mentions paying her debts as late as December 1748, when he records payments totaling £800.[11] Although their marriage was a secret, it was an open secret. In 1747, she had given birth to a son, and while she removed herself to Chelsea for her lying-in, the birth was also widely known in fashionable circles. Afterward, Elizabeth is said to have asked Lord Chesterfield, "Do you know, my Lord, that the world says I have had twins?" In a famous quip, Chesterfield replied, "Does it? For my own part, I make it a point of believing only half of what it says."[12] The baby did not survive its first year, and so the marriage between Elizabeth and Hervey was not betrayed by the introduction of a third person. By that point, relations between the two were so hos-

10 Quoted in Elizabeth Mavor, *The Virgin Mistress: A Study in Survival* (Garden City: Doubleday & Co., 1964), 45.

11 *Augustus Hervey's Journal*, ed. David Erskine (London: William Kimber, 1953), 76. While Hervey's journals cover the years 1746-59, they are a treacherous source of information since he evidently wrote them between 1767 and 1770, years when he had good reason to represent Elizabeth negatively.

12 Mavor, *Virgin Mistress*, 39.

Miss CHUDLEIGH, in the CHARACTER of IPHIGENIA, at the Venetian Ambassador's Masquerade.

Artist Unknown. *Miss Chudleigh, in the Character of Iphigenia, at the Venetian Ambassador's Masquerade*.
Steel engraving. 20.1 x 12.6 cm, plate. In *Horace Walpole and His World*, edited by L. B. Seeley.
London: Seeley, Jackson and Halliday, 1884, volume 4, page [108].

Artist Unknown, after Reynolds. *The Honble. Miss Chudley*. Mezzotint.
34.9 x 24.6 cm, image; 38.1 x 26.3 cm, sheet. In *Horace Walpole and His World*, volume 4, page [129].

tile that Elizabeth's biographers suggest that the child was conceived as a consequence of marital rape.[13] According to Hervey's journals, by 1749 he was finished with
Elizabeth, declaring himself "deaf to all the siren's voice."[14]

Because Hervey had no title and the couple had no issue, the easiest thing to do
was just pretend that their marriage never happened. Apart from the eyewitnesses,
there was no evidence of the marriage, and neither partner had any desire to remain
married. A Parliamentary divorce was prohibitively expensive and could only be
obtained after first proving the marriage they wished to deny, then producing evidence of Elizabeth's adultery. It was a difficult, costly, and public process that neither
of them wanted to pursue. The clandestine nature of their marriage permitted them
just to pretend it never happened.

The informal separation seemed satisfactory to both Elizabeth and Hervey for
nearly two decades. But a new love and social ambition complicated the arrangement
and started Elizabeth down the path that led to the trial at Westminster Hall. First,
in 1748, Elizabeth began an affair with the Duke of Kingston and entertained
thoughts of becoming a duchess. Then, in 1759, Hervey's elder brother, George, was
reported to be near death. This suddenly increased the likelihood that Augustus
would become the Earl of Bristol, and so Elizabeth entertained thoughts of becoming a countess. This situation prompted Elizabeth to undertake a series of extraordinary and illegal acts that made her, for a time, *both* a duchess *and* a countess, a state
of affairs that came back to haunt and (ironically) rescue her in April of 1776.

Elizabeth met Evelyn Pierrepont, the Duke of Kingston, in 1748 at Tunbridge
Wells. He was a handsome and staggeringly wealthy man, and while he was unmarried when he met Elizabeth, he kept a French mistress, Madame de la Touche.[15] By
the summer of 1751, Elizabeth had supplanted Mme de la Touche in the duke's affec-
tions and household. The couple entertained frequently and Elizabeth made liberal
use of the duke's great wealth. But he was a careful man and, knowing her marital
history, he took extraordinary precautions never to be seen engaging in any physical
intimacy with Elizabeth, lest his servants be tempted to tell tales in court should
Augustus Hervey seek a divorce based on her adultery. Such a divorce would be
founded on a successful lawsuit for criminal conversation brought by Hervey against

---

13 Ibid., 37-38; Charles E. Pearce, *The Amazing Duchess*,
   2 vols., 2d ed. (London: Stanley Paul & Co., 1911),
   116-17.

14 *Augustus Hervey's Journal*, 84.

15 The story of the Duke of Kingston's seduction and
   then abandonment of Madame de la Touche is told in

*Les Avantures Trop Amoureuses, ou, Elisabeth Chudleigh
Ex-Duchesse Douairiere de Kingston, aujourd'hui
Comtesse de Bristol, et La Marquise de la Touche sur la
Scene du Monde, Avec d'autres Anecdotes pour servir d'in-
structions à ceux qui en ont besoin & d'amusemens aux
autres* ([Basel?]: aux Depens des Interessez, 1776).

the duke. Such "crim. con." cases could lead to potentially ruinous damage awards, depending on the means of the defendant. The duke's servant, Thomas Whitehead, explains just how careful he was:

> *his Grace being always on his guard, and so extremely cautious, that the twelve years before he married, I never saw him kiss her lips, not even when he took leave of her at Harwich, at her taking shipping for Saxony, to pay a visit to the Electress; nor at her return to England, I being present each time. He took particular care to bolt his chamber-door, on going to bed, either in town or country: indeed, when Miss C— had been at Thoresby, or Pierrepoint-Lodge, the house-maids have frequently brought me a white pocket handkerchief of the Duke's, which they said, with a smile, they found in making her bed. I believe this to be the strongest proof [Hervey] could have obtained, had he sued for a divorce.*[16]

The duke was equally cautious on the question of marriage. Elizabeth wished to avoid becoming a cast-off mistress, like Mme de la Touche, but he sensibly refused to marry unless she could prove herself a single woman in the eyes of the law.

This state of affairs persisted throughout the 1750s, a period when Hervey was regularly out of the country on naval duty. At the end of that decade, Elizabeth got news that George Hervey was seriously ill. Unable to marry the duke, but now perhaps about to become Countess of Bristol upon George's death, Elizabeth determined to secure proof of her clandestine marriage fifteen years earlier. On 11 February 1759, she traveled to Winchester and sought out Mr. Amis, the clergyman who had officiated at her wedding. She found him on his deathbed and, with the advice of a pliant lawyer, persuaded the dying vicar to forge a parish register to record her marriage to Hervey. Now there was documentary evidence (of a sort) of her marriage. Remarkably, when George Hervey recovered his health, dashing her immediate hopes of becoming Countess of Bristol, she never destroyed the register, a careless error she would rue in 1776.

Augustus Hervey retired from the navy in 1763 and became an MP, bringing him in closer proximity to Elizabeth and the duke. They all managed to coexist peacefully until 1768, when Hervey let Elizabeth know through an intermediary that he was

---

16 Thomas Whitehead, *Original Anecdotes of the Late Duke of Kingston and Miss Chudleigh, Alias Mrs. Harvey, alias Countess of Bristol, alias Duchess of Kingston: Interspersed with Memoirs of several of the Nobility and Gentry now living. Written in a Series of Letters to a Gentleman, by Thomas Whitehead, Many Years Servant to the Duke of Kingston, and now Musician at Bath* (London: Printed for S. Blandon, in Paternoster Row, 1792), 6-7.

Artist Unknown. *The married Maid of Honour, or, the Widow'd Wife and her two Husbands.*
Etching & engraving. 17.5 x 11.1 cm, plate. Published by W. Nicholl, 1 February 1775.
In *The Trial of the Duchess of Kingston*, extra-illustrated, following page 17. 775.2.1.3

planning to divorce her. He had a bundle of depositions that he claimed proved her to be an adulteress. Given the duke's caution, these depositions probably refer to adulteries that Elizabeth committed in the 1740s with other men. As early as 1746, Hervey's journal hints that Elizabeth's conduct was "not altogether as Vestal-like" as he wished.[17] A parliamentary divorce would have allowed both of them to remarry, but it would be a major embarrassment for Elizabeth and the duke.

Eager to avoid the scandal of a divorce process, Elizabeth sought an alternative means of extricating herself from her marriage to Hervey that would allow them both to remarry. She found her solution at the Court of Arches, the Ecclesiastical appeals court in London popularly known as Doctors' Commons. On the advice of William Collier, a civilian lawyer who practiced in the court, she initiated a suit of "jactitation of marriage" against Hervey. Jactitation was a little-used process that one party initiated to prevent another from falsely boasting of marriage. With Hervey's collusion, Elizabeth brought the suit against him. Since he could not prove this marriage that he supposedly boasted of, on 10 February 1769, the Court of Arches declared that Elizabeth was single and forbade Hervey to boast of marriage to her. Doctor Collier assured Elizabeth and the Duke of Kingston that this decision allowed them to marry in good conscience and with legal safety. The brazen collusion that produced this legal fiction particularly rankled Elizabeth's prosecutors in 1776 and gave spectators like Anna a very dim view of the integrity of the Court of Arches.

Elizabeth and the duke then took advantage of a loophole in the Hardwicke Marriage Act that permitted them to have, in essence, a clandestine marriage. Instead of publishing the banns and marrying in a public ceremony, they got a special license from the Archbishop of Canterbury, something the Marriage Act permitted in order to preserve the lucrative licensing privileges of the ecclesiastical establishment.[18] The practical effect of the Archbishop's Special License was to allow the head of the church to help the rich and powerful evade the law, and to collect a fee for doing so.[19] Elizabeth became the Duchess of Kingston on 8 March 1769 in a hasty and quiet ceremony in the duke's dressing room in his house in Arlington Street, Westminster. According to Thomas Whitehead, who witnessed the ceremony, it was as rushed and secret an affair as her first marriage.[20]

---

17 *Augustus Hervey's Journal*, 41.

18 Outhwaite, *Clandestine Marriage*, 79-80.

19 Critics of the Marriage Act of 1753 took special aim at the licensing provisions. For criticism of the Archbishop's Special License, see *Some Considerations on* the *Act to Prevent Clandestine Marriages, in a Letter from a Gentleman of the Temple, to the Lord B[ishop] of L[ondon]* (London, 1754), 16.

20 Whitehead, *Original Anecdotes*, 12-13.

Elizabeth had now achieved her ambition of becoming a peeress: she was both a duchess and one of the richest women in Europe. While she spent freely, her life with the duke was not as ostentatious as one might expect. Whitehead remembers that they enjoyed decidedly unfashionable pastimes, such as fishing together when in the country and attending the trials before Sir John Fielding at Bow Street when in town. The idea of Elizabeth and the duke being amused by watching other people on trial is, of course, a great irony given the fate that awaited her. She might have avoided her own embarrassing trial for bigamy had the duke not rewritten his will on 5 July 1770. In that will, he left everything to Elizabeth during her lifetime (provided she did not remarry), then gave the real estate to his nephew, Charles Meadows, after her death. This specifically disinherited the eldest brother of the Meadows family, Evelyn. Exactly why the duke disinherited Evelyn Meadows is something of a mystery. In Anna's observations on the trial, she suggests that Meadows earned the duke's enmity by leaving the army "ignobly," then compounded his offense by not fulfilling his engagements to a Miss Bishop. Anna calls Meadows a "vile Man" and says, "I am sure the Devil has marked him for his own."

The Duke of Kingston died on 23 September 1773 and his will was probated on 1 October. Evelyn Meadows, finding he was disinherited, immediately began making inquiries into Elizabeth's past, hoping to prove her bigamy and invalidate the will. By chance, he kept his horses at stables maintained by John Fozard, a former servant of the Duke of Kingston. Fozard connected Meadows to servants who could help his case. Amazingly, this included the widow of Mr. Amis, the parson who married Elizabeth to Augustus Hervey. After Amis's death, his widow married a Mr. Phillips, the duke's steward at his estate at Thoresby. With her help, Meadows learned of the phony registry that Amis made and was able to obtain it. She also put Meadows in touch with Anne Craddock, the servant who witnessed the marriage in 1744.[21]

On 8 December 1774, a Grand Jury for the County of Middlesex indicted Elizabeth for bigamy. If she did not answer the charge, she would be declared an outlaw, exposing her estate to seizure by the Crown. Elizabeth was in Rome at the time of the indictment and had to make a dangerous trans-Alpine crossing during winter in order to answer the charges in England. She made her way to Calais by late March, but then remained there for eight weeks, fearful that if she went to England, she would be arrested and imprisoned. During this period, she huddled with her lawyers and even received a visit from Lord Mansfield, who assured her that she would not

21 Mavor, *Virgin Mistress*, 109-11.

be molested when she arrived in England. Having received these assurances, she left Calais for England in May 1775 to answer the charges.

As a duchess, Elizabeth exercised her privilege of requesting that her case be heard by a jury of her peers, which meant the peers of the realm, the House of Lords. Throughout the fall of 1775, the Lords made preparations for the trial, which was to begin in December. In fact, the trial did not begin until the following April, due to delays occasioned by Elizabeth's falling ill and by the increasingly elaborate preparations the Lords felt were necessary for the trial. The case had acquired great symbolic value and it preoccupied the House of Lords at the very moment when a shooting war started in the American colonies. Indeed, the only value the case had was symbolic. The duke's will was written in such a way as to protect Elizabeth's inheritance even if her bigamy were proved. Furthermore, Augustus Hervey had become the Earl of Bristol in March 1775, so if Elizabeth was not a duchess, she would still be a countess. As such, she could claim benefit of clergy and avoid punishment for her crime, which was death.[22] According to J. M. Beattie, by the fourteenth century the benefit of clergy had become "a massive fiction that tempered in practice the harshness of the common law rule that virtually all felonies were capital offenses."[23] Benefit of clergy was gradually extended to women in the seventeenth century, making it available to Elizabeth a century later. Knowing that Elizabeth would claim this benefit if convicted, Lord Mansfield reasonably asked during a debate in the House of Lords, "*Cui bono?* What utility is to be obtained, suppose a conviction be the result? The lady makes your Lordships a *curtsey*, and you return a *bow*."[24] But reason and utility were beside the point; the Duchess of Kingston was going to be tried for bigamy in spectacular fashion.

Before that trial started, everyone involved knew it would end in a conviction and that Elizabeth would suffer no penalty. But the process was not entirely pointless. Indeed, there were many points to be made by trying Elizabeth in so grand and public a manner. First, the case would illustrate the corruptions of the Ecclesiastical Court system that those involved in the Common Law courts thought had become scandalous. The trial was as much a showdown between these competing court systems as it was between Evelyn Meadows and Elizabeth.

---

22 According to Stone, *Road to Divorce*, 143, convicted bigamists were not put to death in the eighteenth century; rather, they were branded on the thumb. By the 1760s, the brand was rarely even heated, and in the 1790s the penalty changed to transportation for seven years.

23 J. M. Beattie, *Crime and the Courts in England, 1660-1800* (Princeton: Princeton University Press, 1986), 141.

24 *An Authentic Detail of Particulars Relative to the Late Duchess of Kingston. The Third Edition, With Considerable Additions* (London, 1790), 77.

Artist Unknown. *Duchess of Kingston*. Stipple engraving & etching
with detail showing a rare side view of the courtroom. 13.7 x 8.1 cm,
image; 15.1 x 9.8 cm, sheet. Published by James Cundee, 10 April 1807.

Second, the trial allowed the House of Lords to publicize the dangers of clandestine marriage, bigamy, and wifely adultery to the political establishment. For decades, the House of Lords had tried to reform the marriage laws in order to prevent the children of noble families—their children—from marrying without parental consent. Until 1753, these efforts were always frustrated by Commons, whose members were more sympathetic to social advancement through marriage—the MPs, like Henry Fox, were the ones hoping to seduce the daughters of peers, as he did when he married Lady Georgiana Caroline Lennox in a clandestine ceremony.[25] Even after passage of the Hardwicke Marriage Act, some in Commons sought to amend and repeal the law. Elizabeth's bigamy allowed the Lords to show the continuing threat to lineal descent of property and title even after the reforms of 1753.

The third, and most important, point to the trial was to sacrifice Elizabeth as a scapegoat for the sexual indiscretions of the upper class. During the 1770s, the sexual misbehavior of the "better sort" had been publicly exposed as never before. The decade started with the Earl of Grosvenor's crim. con. suit against the Duke of Cumberland, brother of George III. Grosvenor won an award of £10,000 and the royal family was acutely embarrassed by the details of the case. Those details were published in a number of trial reports, helping to transform adultery trial reports into a mildly pornographic genre.[26] While salacious trial reports were not new in the 1770s, they became increasingly oriented toward attacking aristocratic privilege at this time.[27] This was also the decade when the *Town and Country Magazine* began publishing its "tête-à-tête" column, a regular feature that retailed rumors of the sex lives of famous people. Among those featured in "tête-à-tête" were Solicitor General John Dunning and Attorney General Edward Thurloe, two of Elizabeth's prosecutors.[28] (Of course, the Duke of Cumberland was one of her jurors.) Fashionable London turned out for Elizabeth's trial in the hopes that her sacrifice would wash away their sins.

25 Outhwaite, *Clandestine Marriage*, 70-72.

26 Stone, *Road to Divorce*, 44, calls divorce proceedings the "soft core pornography of the late eighteenth century." See also David M. Turner, *Fashioning Adultery: Gender, Sex and Civility in England 1660-1740* (Cambridge: Cambridge University Press, 2002), ch. 6; and Peter Wagner, "The Pornographer in the Courtroom: Trial Reports about Cases of Sexual Crimes and Delinquencies as a Genre of Eighteenth-Century Erotica," in *Sexuality in Eighteenth-Century Britain*,

ed. Paul Gabriel Bouce (Manchester: Manchester University Press, 1982), 120-40.

27 See Donna T. Andrew, "'Adultery-à-Mode': Privilege, the Law and Attitudes to Adultery 1770-1809," *History* 82 (1997): 5-23.

28 For the story of Dunning's liaison with a prostitute, Miss Lucy C—n, see *Town and Country Magazine* 6 (December 1774): 625-27; for Thurloe's liaison with "the Temple Toast," see *Town and Country Magazine* 4 (November 1772): 568-71.

Artist Unknown. *The Temple Toast   The Amorous Advocate [Attorney General Edward Thurloe].*
Engraving. 10.5 x 17.5 cm, plate. Published in *Town and Country Magazine,*
volume 4, facing page 569, January 1772. 772.11.0.4

Artist Unknown. *Miss C_____   The Powerfull Pleader [Solicitor General John Dunning].*
Etching & engraving. 10.5 x 17.5 cm, plate. Published in *Town and Country Magazine,*
volume 6, facing page 625, by A. Hamilton, January 1775. 775.1.1.3

Anna's observations on the trial comment on each of these three important motivations. What makes her commentary special is that she discusses these reasons for the trial, but has no personal stake in any of them. While no champion of Elizabeth, Anna does not revel in the scapegoating. Instead, she offers detailed, shrewd, and even-handed observations on the trial and its main issues. The different accounts she wrote of the trial reveal a great deal about the event itself, but they are just as interesting for what they reveal about their author.

II. The Lewis Walpole Library Manuscripts

The Lewis Walpole Library manuscripts are the only early manuscripts by Anna known to have survived. We know that there were early journals because the first volume of her seventeen-volume diary, preserved in the Henry E. Huntington Library, is a compendium of her journals from 1773 to 1786. She called this initial volume her "Methodized Journal" because she methodically reduced her earlier writings into a single volume. In a headnote, she describes her method:

> *My method from fifteen years of age was, to write down every Evening what persons, I had seen, books read, sentiments heard in the day &c. I observed much: talked little. At first these journalic notes were extremely concise— by degrees fuller, but always roughly taken; I have reviewed all my yearly books, & merely have methodized my hurried entries— scarcely altering a word— never the sense.*

Not surprisingly, this disavowal of self-censorship has been greeted skeptically by scholars. For one thing, the "Methodized Journal" is dedicated to her sister and husband in a manner that suggests an acute anxiety over any possible breaches of morality it might contain. She invites them to "Praise me where you can. Condemn me where you must: But LOVE me every where if you can." The Lewis Walpole Library manuscripts are almost certainly part of the "yearly books" she used to compile the "Methodized Journal." As such, they allow us to see how truthful her claim in the headnote is by comparing what she thought fit to tell her husband and sister, at the age of twenty-eight or older, to what she thought fit to tell her female friends when she was an unmarried eighteen-year-old.

The entry in the "Methodized Journal" is a marvel of concision. In fewer than two hundred words, she sums up the entire trial:

This year attended the Dss of Kingston's extraordinary trial for Bigamy &c. &c. April the 15. went with Lady Bathurst in the Ld. High Stewards box— the trial began by the Duchess's reply to her inditement. The Attorney General Thurlow opened the cause— the defendants Council pleaded the sentence of the Ecclesiastical Court against the trial. April 16. Attended in the Gallery belonging to the Board of Works.— the Council for the prosecution replied. Thurlow, Wedderburne, Dunning & Harris ably. the trial adjourned to the 19th.— On that day I went again. Thurlow was applied to by Wallace— he drew up a Statement of the Evidences to be produced, one witness examined to prove the fact.— The 22. I attended the trial again; which on that day was concluded.— the Prisoner read her defence— the witnesses for her examined. She was declared Guilty unanimously except the Duke of Newcastle, not intentionally Guilty— She pleaded her peerage.— After a long pleading against her plea & a longer reply by her council— it was admitted her next offence was to be deemed Capital— she paid the fees.

She mentions the names of the prosecutors, briefly touches on some parts of the process, and tells us where she sat. But as the tantalizing ampersands in the first sentence suggest, there is more to her recollections about the trial.

The Lewis Walpole Library manuscripts are two related documents. The first is a six-page letter to a friend named Gertrude. This letter was composed piecemeal over the course of the trial in Richardsonian style, literally written "to the moment." The dateline on the first page of the letter says "Monday morning 7 O'Clock." In the early morning hours before the trial began, Anna wrote:

I can absolutely settle to nothing.— No Chaos ever equalled my head at present, & I will venture to pronounce the heads of half the People in this great Town. This day the Duchess of Kingston is tried for Bigamy— the whole Town has talked of nothing else, for this week past. . . . I [have been?] up since 5 O'Clock— attending my Hairdresser 'tho we do [not?] leave this house this half hour. I shall give you a most ample History of the whole as I go through with it every day.

In contrast to her "methodized" entry, this letter begins with Anna's head in chaos, yet newly dressed. She promises not a summary, but a "most ample History."

The history she provides for Gertrude is written with a good sense of audience and focuses mostly on the excitement of the trial as a social event. From a coffeehouse adjoining Westminster Hall, Anna waited with Lady Bathurst's party on that first

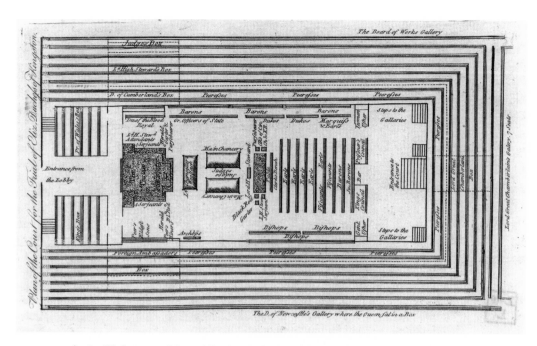

Artist Unknown. *Plan of the Court for the Trial of Eliz. Duchess of Kingston.*
Etching & engraving. 21.2 x 13.2 cm, sheet.

morning and enjoyed "seeing the Peers & Peeresses coming into the Hall from their Carriages, which were mostly elegant ones, & the Horses full harnessd & ornamented." Once inside the hall, she saw that "the first Coup d'Œil of the Hall filled with well dressed people was extreamly striking, the Peers were scattered about, & we waited an hour before the Procession came in." A correspondent to the *Public Ledger* confirms Anna's description of the well-dressed crowd when he describes how the ladies on the east side of the hall shone brilliantly in the afternoon sunlight because of the profusion of jewels they wore.[29]

The most striking element of the first day was the grand procession of peers into the hall. It was performed with great ceremony and involved scores of attendants. The procession was particularly important to Anna because her brother, George, was one of the twenty young men who bore the Lord High Steward's train. She devotes over five hundred words to the procession alone, more than twice the length of the entry in the "Methodized Journal." Indeed, the procession was one of the highlights of the trial for everyone. Hannah More called it "a sight which, for beauty and magnificence, exceeded anything which those who were never present at a coronation, or a trial by peers, can have the least notions of."[30] An anonymous pamphlet entitled *Ceremonial for the Trial of a Peer* was published just before the trial. Like a

29 *Public Ledger*, 16 April 1776.

30 *The Letters of Hannah More*, ed. R. Brimley Johnson (London: John Lane The Bodley Head, 1925), 41.

ELIZABETH *Dutchess Dowager of* KINGSTON.
Taken at the Bar of the House of Lords, on the 15 of April 1776.
Publish'd as the Act directs, May 20, 1776.

Taylor. *Elizabeth Dutchess Dowager of Kingston.*
Mezzotint. 37.7 x 27.8 cm, sheet. Published 20 May 1776. 776.5.20.2

playbill, it described the order in which the peers and their attendants would enter the hall, and it included a diagram of the "stage" on which Elizabeth would be tried. Anna and many of the spectators probably had copies of this little book in hand as the procession took place. Given the detailed description she gave to Gertrude two days later, she may have consulted it when writing her letter.

This grand procession was an appropriate way to begin a trial that was generally regarded to be more a theatrical than a legal event. Processions had been very popular dumb show entertainments at Drury Lane and Covent Garden during the previous decade.[31] Indeed, the theatrical nature of Elizabeth's trial is hard to overstate— and it was not just the lords who were performing for the crowd. When Elizabeth entered the hall, she staged a procession of her own. It included three female attendants in white dresses, two chaplains, and an apothecary. Anna describes Elizabeth's appearance in great detail:

> *Then entered the renowned Duchess . . . her train borne— her dress was [suitable?] to the occasion, all Black:—A Black silk negligée on not a large Hoop—Black Crape Ruffles, not a speck of white discerned—her hair dressed, & a long Black hood most becomingly put on.—It came down in a point before to her forehead, & being [wired?] out, & falling on her shoulders was exactly the headdress of Mary Queen of Scots in the old Pictures. . . . Her aspect was unconcerned, seemingly unaffectedly so—she really looked handsome.*

The description is mostly devoted to Elizabeth's dress, which caught the attention of many commentators. Anna's comparison of Elizabeth to Mary, Queen of Scots, is significant in light of the romanticization of Mary during the eighteenth century. Elizabeth may have dressed with the intention to evoke sympathetic associations between her and the tragic queen. The growing interest in Mary Stuart led to a vigorous market in portraits of her. Many of these paintings were of dubious authenticity, as Horace Walpole knew, but they were evidently well known.[32] The common element among them was Mary's black costume, specifically the "Mary Stuart cap."[33]

31 At the time of George III's coronation, Drury Lane included a fancy royal procession in performances of *Henry VIII*. Called *The Coronation*, the procession was frequently repeated during the season. After the Shakespeare Jubilee of 1769, both Drury Lane and Covent Garden offered competing processions of famous Shakespeare characters.

32 *The Correspondence of Horace Walpole*, vol. 42, *Horace Walpole's Miscellaneous Correspondence III*, ed. W. S. Lewis and John Riely with the assistance of Edwine A. Martz and Ruth K. McClure (New Haven: Yale University Press, 1980), 320-22.

33 Roy Strong, *Tudor and Jacobean Portraits*, 2 vols. (London: Her Majesty's Stationery Office, 1969), 222.

Artist Unknown. *Iphigenia's late procession from Kingston to Bristol.—by Chudleigh Meadows.*
Etching. 32.3 x 40.2 cm, plate. 15 April 1776. Published by Charles Bathurst, London, 1776.
In *The Trial of the Duchess of Kingston*, extra-illustrated, following page 16. 776.4.15.1.2

If Elizabeth sought to dress as the tragic queen during her trial, some commentators had a different costume in mind. The title of one print of Elizabeth's procession—"Iphigenia's late procession from Kingston to Bristol"—reminds the audience that she did not always choose to appear in such decorous clothes. Appropriate to Elizabeth's histrionic entrance, Anna describes her in theatrical terms, even to the point of suspecting her of acting. Elizabeth is "seemingly unaffectedly" unconcerned by the trial, but Anna clearly doubts her sincerity.

The details of the trial are passed over very quickly in the letter to Gertrude. Instead of discussing the testimony of witnesses and points of law, Anna devotes only about five hundred words to a bare-bones description of the trial itself, the same amount of space she dedicated to the procession alone. The purpose of this letter was to allow Gertrude vicariously to enjoy the fashionable spectacle of the trial. For that reason, it focuses on descriptions of dress, processions, and handsome lawyers: "Do you know [Attorney General] Thurloe? He has such a Tongue! & such sensible Eyes! that he may plead any cause even to a Lady.—but I am a mere rattle just now."

At the end of this high-spirited letter, Anna looks forward to a much different kind of document. She asks Gertrude to return the letter so that she can use it to help her memory as she prepares "an account of the [whole?] proceedings, which I will send you, 'tho I make no doubt the Trial will be published, how ever the production of a female Pen may be most pleasing to a Female reader." The account she refers to constitutes the second, much longer, of the two Lewis Walpole Library manuscripts. This document, which runs to thirty-two pages, is written in a neat hand and has a formal title: "A Short Account of the Proceedings on the Trial of the Duchess Dowager of Kingston for Bigamy before the Lord High Steward & her Peers in Westminster Hall—Commenced on the 15th of April, 1776." Like the letter to Gertrude, it is written specifically for a "Female reader" by a "female Pen," but the two documents could hardly be more different in their style and content. The former deals with the manner of the trial, the latter deals more with the matter. The letter is informal, chatty, and private, while the "Short Account" is a more formal, serious, and quasi-public document.

To understand the importance of what Anna attempted in the "Short Account," we first need to consider her attitudes toward women's writing. Looking at Anna's later journals, John Brewer and Claire Miller Colombo have shown that she normally refuses to encroach upon subjects that were conventionally the preserve of men. In particular, she hesitates to state her own opinions about nonfiction books and public affairs. By contrast, she was not apologetic when judging the quality of sermons she had heard or imaginative literature she had read—and she was frequently a tough critic. Because Anna discusses conventionally "feminine" material, but refuses to discuss "masculine" subjects like politics and the law, Colombo concludes that Anna is practicing self-censorship and places the blame squarely on the influence of her husband, the government censor.[34] But we see these same concerns with feminine propriety in Anna's "Short Account," written long before she met John Larpent. This suggests that Anna's desire to write about her culture was always

34 Colombo, "Public Performance," 286.

tempered by a strong internalized conviction that certain subjects were not proper for women to discuss.

What makes the "Short Account" significant is that Anna finds a way to address the "masculine" topics that she generally avoided in her later journals. She does this in three ways. First, she limits her readership to women. At the end of her letter to Gertrude, she promises that the "Short Account" will be the product of a "female Pen" created for a "Female reader." Second, she consistently (and, one suspects, disingenuously) undercuts her own judgment when she comments on the substance of the legal issues in the trial. Every time she explains the legal process, she follows her explanation with an apology for venturing into matters that she claims not to understand. Third, she circulates the account in manuscript instead of trying to publish it. In the letter to Gertrude, she specifically distinguishes her promised account from the inevitable published reports of the trial, written by men.

Brewer notes that although Anna was immersed in texts all her life and had very strong opinions about her culture, she never ventured into print.[35] While she admired the work of female writers, she could never bring herself to expose her writing to the buying public. And yet, the "Short Account" seems to be an attempt to compete with those published, male-authored accounts, albeit among a limited, female audience. In this sense, the "Short Account" functions in the same way that Colombo says the later journals do: as a genre that allowed Anna safely to "enter into public discourse."[36]

Everywhere in the "Short Account" one can see evidence of Anna's negotiations between the desire to be a proper lady and the desire to be a public commentator. In several instances, she reports with lucidity and accuracy on the specific matters of law being discussed. The first day of the trial was devoted to arguments about whether the Court of Arches's ruling in the jactitation suit were subject to review by the House of Lords, acting as a Common Law court. Anna writes:

> *I should have mention'd that each Council founded the impossibility of bringing on the trial, on a statute of Henry the 8th by which all sentences given by the Ecclesiastical Court were deemed final & decisive in all cases whatsoever; this was a great road to all the Law of the land; very edifying to those who understood it but you will not be surprized when I say I was not able to retain enough to repeat it intelligibly to you.*

35 Brewer, "Reconstructing," 232.
36 Colombo, "Public Performance," 291.

Despite this last disclaimer, Anna is clear and specific about the major point of contention at the outset of the trial. She obviously understood the substance, but she appeals to her audience's (and her own) prejudice against a woman's taking too keen an interest in such matters.

Frequently, Anna distinguishes between the legal matters discussed and the manner in which they were presented, reinforcing the notion that law is a man's world, style a woman's. For example, she discusses John Dunning's delivery in great detail:

> *To an exceeding bad person is joined the false conviction of being perfectly handsome. Imagine the ridiculous composition this forms!—Imagine that composition appearing at a grave & solemn Bar!—& thence conclude that imagination cannot design a more ridiculous object.—A voice nearly ahstmatic accompany'd with a constant, hollow, Cough.—At the end of every period comes a Cough.—At the beginning a hem.—Oh! the agreeable Oratour.—But let us leave __manner__ & dwell on the __matter__ it so ill expressed.— Here I own myself no judge.*

While Anna was sympathetic to the prosecution, she is highly critical of Dunning, one of the prosecutors. Again, we see her making no excuses for judging Dunning's *manner*, but she apologizes when she turns to the legal *matter* by claiming that she is no judge of the substance. By contrast, Hannah More also considered Dunning "insufferably bad, coughing and spitting at every three words," but she commends his "sense and his expression pointed to the last degree; he made her grace shed bitter tears."[37]

Anna excused herself from the fourth day of the trial for fear that the witness testimony that day would not just be something a lady could not properly judge, but something a lady could not properly hear. She explains:

> *Saturday the 20th I did not attend; but my Brother did. I can therefore repeat from him what passed in order to carry on the Thread of the Tale.— My nonattendance proceeded from my imagining the Evidences would be rather unfit for a Female Ear.—I was disappointed, for I suppose no Trial of such a stamp was carry'd on with the Delicate Decency this was.*

37 *Letters of Hannah More*, 41. The low opinion of Dunning's oratory is shared by the author of *Characters. Containing an Impartial Review of the Public Conduct* and *Abilities of the most Eminent Personages in the Parliament of Great Britain* (London, 1777), 110-11.

Artist Unknown. *Representation of the Trial of the Dutchess of Kingston.*
Etching & engraving. 20.8 x 12.6 cm, sheet.

While she wishes to hear all that happened, she does not wish *to be seen* hearing all that happened. Anna obviously felt comfortable attending a trial about bigamy and the manipulation of marriage laws, subjects that eighteenth-century periodicals categorized as relating to the "fair sex," but the prospect of testimony about sex acts was more than she could decently face.[38] Her disappointment arises from the absence of scandalous matter: she skipped a day at the trial for no good reason.

On the final day of the trial, Elizabeth spoke in her own defense. Significantly, Anna's reluctance to criticize the content of the lawyers' arguments did not extend to Elizabeth's personal legal defense. When she read a carefully prepared statement, Anna felt free to pass judgment:

> *Upon that the Duchess rose to make her defence. It consisted of 13 sheets of Law Paper—not very Coherent nor very Elegant, but her situation; the* <u>*tout ensemble*</u>*; rendered it interesting.—She began by setting forth her Ancestry. Poor Woman. We all sprang from Adam & perhaps she might particularly be stiled one of Eves Daughters if frailty marked the immediate Parentage!*

When a woman presumes to speak thirteen sheets of law in public, Anna makes no apologies for passing judgment on it. Indeed, she devotes over eight hundred words to her summary of Elizabeth's defense and makes many editorial comments on it. After relating that Elizabeth disclaimed love of riches and titles, Anna exclaims, "Oh Woman! Woman! How Could you utter such untruths!" Commenting on Elizabeth's plea that the lords believe she thought herself innocent when she married the duke, Anna writes, "She read the rest but repeated that from memory & shewed her power in the Pathetic, indeed I never saw a better actress."

These criticisms are not surprising. Elizabeth was a notorious woman in the eyes of most of her contemporaries, but she was particularly obnoxious to Anna because she embodied two of the qualities that, according to Brewer, Anna frequently criticized in her later journals: bad morals and social climbing.[39] But unlike many other commentators, Anna is not wholly unsympathetic to Elizabeth's predicament. Brewer notes another quality characteristic of Anna that we see in the "Short Account." She liked to have her sympathy excited, but only if there were a moral. Colombo agrees, observing that Anna enjoyed plays and imaginative literature, but only if that diversion also brought moral improvement.[40]

---

38 See Kathryn Shevelow, *Women and Print Culture: The Construction of Femininity in the Early Periodical* (London and New York: Routledge, 1989).

39 Brewer, "Reconstructing," 232.
40 Colombo, "Public Performance," 295.

Anna found herself both entertained and edified by the trial. We see this during her relation of the moment of highest drama in the courtroom. On the last day of the trial, when Elizabeth found her case was truly hopeless, she fell into a hysterical fit that greatly affected Anna. She describes the scene at length:

> *the struggle of passion long stifled, every heart breaking consideration aris-ing; worked on the Prisoner's mind & occasion'd one of the most shocking Fits I ever saw or could conceive.—It stopp'd the Court & She was carry'd out.—I frankly own that I never was more affected, that very wickedness that prevents most people from feeling for this miserable Woman, in my mind added to the horror of her situation.—When distress assaults, virtue is our only cordial. What a Chaos is the mind without it, & with the stings of vice added to every other grief.—Sensibility is not an inhabitant of her breast, but disappointed Ambition & humiliating guilt are dreadful harpies.—It shocked me to see that most of the Women Spectators called her an Actress & were entertained with her situation.—'Tis Strange that we are generally the hardest on the errors of our own Sex,—a narrowness of mind which I hope proceeds only from the too frequent narrowness of educa-tion given many women. The want of reflexion & of an early use of com-bining causes with effects—by which the evil of those effects may be softened, when we see the springs of them; the Temptations to them; & consider the frailty of human nature.—This is a long digression. My heart & Pen are in such Unison that as I really made these reflexions whilst the Lords adjourned to their House to debate on what punishment should be inflicted on her, I give them in this place.*

This description, ostensibly about Elizabeth's hysterical fit, actually focuses more on Anna's reaction to it. While a tough critic of Elizabeth's morals, Anna at least refrains from kicking her when she was, literally, down. The fit Elizabeth suffered was affecting in itself, but what Anna finds more shocking is the unsympathetic reac-tion of the other female spectators. Elizabeth is a bad woman who has no "virtue" to serve as a "cordial" in her distress, and the laughter of the other women only exacer-bates the "horror" of Elizabeth's situation. For these reasons, Anna responds with "Sensibility," a reaction that Elizabeth and the other ladies in the hall are not capable of because of the narrowness of their education. Anna chastises the other women for being merely diverted by the "actress," a word she previously applied to Elizabeth when commenting on her personal defense. In this instance, however, Anna seems to believe that Elizabeth's fit is genuine. Ironically, Anna's own words sound very much like a theatrical review of the didactic, sympathetic drama she enjoyed. She describes the action on stage then explains her own exemplary, sympathetic response to it.

Anna's comments also point to a more fundamental anxiety about the relation between language and truth. As if to refute any objections that her words are not the genuine, unmediated translation of her feelings, she assures the reader, "My heart & Pen are in such Unison that as I really made these reflexions whilst the Lords adjourned to their House to debate on what punishment should be inflicted on her, I give them in this place." By contrast, Elizabeth's words have a much different relation to truth. Her "13 sheets of Law Paper" not only represent an unladylike intrusion into a masculine domain, but they are merely "sheets of Law," and nothing else. The material specificity of that phrase suggests that those pages, which should be a synecdoche for Elizabeth's innocence, do not have a real-world referent because Elizabeth was not innocent, as everybody knew. Instead, Elizabeth's existence as the Duchess of Kingston was merely a legal fiction. It existed only in her "sheets of Law" and the Court of Arches's ruling in the jactitation suit. Indeed, as Anna notes, Elizabeth's counsel admitted the collusion used to obtain that ruling, but argued that although a fiction, it was a *legal fiction*, sanctioned by a court that the House of Lords had no authority to question.

This is a highly significant moment when we see Anna making a distinction between licit and illicit female discourse. Elizabeth spoke in a law court before four thousand spectators, whereas Anna speaks to a private circle of female companions. Elizabeth sought to preserve the legal fiction of the Duchess of Kingston by papering over her bigamy. By contrast, Anna wants her readers to see neither paper nor pen, but the genuine "Sensibility" that flows directly from her sympathetic heart to her readers.

And yet, because Anna left three different accounts of the trial, we can see that the relation between truth and language is a very tricky one in this instance. The "Methodized Journal" omits any mention of Elizabeth's courtroom fit and Anna's sympathetic reaction to it. The letter to Gertrude mentions the fit only as an afterthought: "I should have told you that The Duchess had a most horrid fit the last day, which made a sad hub bub in the Hall; I never saw any thing more shocking, she was carry'd out, & the proceeding stopped for half an hour." There is no description of the strong emotions Anna experienced during that half hour, and the phrase "sad hub bub" seems almost to make light of the event.

What becomes clear when we compare Anna's three versions of the trial is her skill as a rhetorician. Each document has a different audience and purpose, and in each case, she tailors the material and her ethos to suit her rhetorical goals. The letter to Gertrude begins amid the excitement of the first morning of the trial and seeks to recreate the atmosphere by focusing on spectacular elements like the initial procession. The "Short Account" is an altogether more ambitious document. It combines the legal details of a published trial report with descriptions of the lawyers' delivery and the defendant's demeanor that one might find in a personal letter. Added to this is the sort of personal reflection appropriate to a diary entry. As a result, the "Short Account" is an especially thorough and scrupulous description of the whole process that greatly enhances our knowledge about the trial. The entry in the "Methodized Journal," by contrast, is a highly sanitized and condensed version of the trial written later in life. It is an emotionless relation of the fact that Anna attended this important event and had a good seat on the first day, but it reveals little else. Given the disclaimer in the headnote to the "Methodized Journal" that Anna did not alter the substance of her source material, one would never know just how much she withheld from her husband and sister.

III. Conclusion

When the trial was over, Elizabeth left the courtroom as the Countess of Bristol. Her new title allowed her to avoid any punishment by pleading benefit of clergy. Although the Lords adjourned to their house privately to discuss the propriety of granting a woman benefit of clergy, there was little doubt that they would consent to it. After the trial, Lord Camden confided to Hannah More that he thought Elizabeth ought to have suffered the indignity of a cold brand (the traditional punishment for bigamy at that time was to touch the hand with a cold branding iron), but he thought it would be ungallant for him to propose this, given that he and Elizabeth were former lovers.[41] And so, as Lord Mansfield predicted the previous fall, Elizabeth curtseyed to her peers and walked out of the magnificent courtroom unpunished. This was a great disappointment to George Colman the Younger and his friends at the Westminster School who had hoped to see Elizabeth publicly whipped.[42] She left England that night and lived the rest of her life on the Continent, traveling between Rome, Calais, Paris, and St. Petersburg. Despite Evelyn Meadows's best efforts, he was never able to wrestle her inheritance away from her. Instead, she spent the Duke of Kingston's money freely, buying several houses and,

41 *Letters of Hannah More*, 45.
42 Richard Brinsley Peake, *Memoirs of the Colman Family*, 2 vols. (London: Bentley, 1841), 1: 410.

among other things, establishing an experimental farm in Russia. She died in Paris in 1788, a naturalized French citizen.

However infamous and reviled Elizabeth was in her own lifetime, her press since has improved greatly. Charles E. Pearce's 1911 biography, *The Amazing Duchess*, seeks to reverse the negative historical judgment of his subject. He praises Elizabeth's "indomitable courage" and "superabundant energy and spirits."[43] Similarly, Elizabeth Mavor is skeptical of the "conventional picture" of Elizabeth. In *The Virgin Mistress* of 1964, Mavor's sympathy for her subject leads her to regard Elizabeth's exploits as an inspiring study in survival.[44] And most recently, Claire Gervat's *Elizabeth: The Scandalous Life of the Duchess of Kingston* of 2003 also champions its subject.[45] This reassessment of Elizabeth's motives and importance is dubious, but the modern biographers at least have attempted to understand Elizabeth as more than just a "bad woman."

In contrast to Elizabeth, Anna remained a respectable, pious lady until her death. Her journals show that she was an extremely well-read woman who remained interested in her culture throughout her life. As L. W. Conolly has demonstrated, she was an avid fan of the theatre and sometimes took a very active role in helping her husband censor play and opera texts.[46] But despite her manifest desire to play an active role in her culture as a critic and censor, she retained a fundamentally conservative view of women's participation in the public sphere. Jeffrey N. Cox calls her a "Phyllis Schlafly of the Romantic era," a woman who "wielded a power she would have denied to other women."[47] But this is an overly harsh judgment. While Anna seems never to have reconciled her intellectual ambitions to her moral beliefs, The Lewis Walpole Library manuscripts reveal her to be more sensitive and conflicted about her views than Cox's characterization suggests.

First, the manuscripts show us that Anna attended the trial to participate in a sensational public event and to understand both the issues at law and the defendant's emotional predicament. She was also motivated by a desire to share the experience with her female readers and explain the legal issues to them. The dual motives of pleasure and instruction contrast strongly with the detached hauteur of Horace Wal-

43 Pearce, *Amazing Duchess*, 14-15.
44 Other twentieth-century biographies include: Muriel Elwood, *The Bigamous Duchess: A Romantic Biography of Elizabeth Chudleigh, Duchess of Kingston* (Indianapolis: Bobbs-Merrill, 1960); and Doris Leslie, *The Incredible Duchess: The Life and Times of Elizabeth Chudleigh* (London: Heinemann, 1974).

45 Claire Gervat, *Elizabeth: The Scandalous Life of the Duchess of Kingston* (London: Century, 2003).
46 *The Censorship of English Drama, 1737-1824* (San Marino: Huntington Library, 1976), 41-42 and 111.
47 Cox, "Romanticism," 42.

pole and the nastiness of Hannah More, who seems to have attended the trial with the sole intention of ridiculing as many people as possible. While More relishes Elizabeth's "bitter tears," Anna provides a thoughtful digression about how narrowness of education leads women to attack each other. One is tempted to detect a faint adumbration of Wollstonecraft in that passage, not Phyllis Schlafly.

Second, the manuscripts constitute the only extended narrative of the trial told from a woman's point of view. The details Anna provides go well beyond the published accounts, which are characterized by a legalistic relation of the process and transcription of the speeches of counsel.[48] Anna offers an enormous amount of detail about the atmosphere of the proceedings and the courtroom styles of the lawyers, lords, witnesses, and defendant. The excerpts I have reproduced above constitute a fraction of the entire account. It is a rich and valuable supplement to the printed accounts that must be read in full to be appreciated.

Finally, the manuscripts presented here allow us to judge how radically different her source material could be from the shape it takes in her "Methodized Journal." They confirm Colombo's suspicion that (at least in this instance) Anna drastically altered her early journals when creating the "Methodized Journal." But the habit of negotiating between proper and improper subjects and forms of literary expression preceded Anna's marriage to John Larpent. She did not learn to "censor" herself after marrying the censor; rather, she struggled in creative ways to give public voice to her opinions, albeit short of venturing into print. The Lewis Walpole Library manuscripts poignantly demonstrate the intellectual ambitions that she felt at an early age but would not pursue because she considered them to be inconsistent with her gender. In the postscript to the letter to Gertrude, Anna addresses this subject in a humorous way, but perhaps with a wistful undertone in the joke:

> P. S. A month ago I raved about _Chapeaux plumied_ & fine Men, I now am in love with nothing but long wigs, gowns, & bands; as to Mr. Thurloe (the Attorney general) I think or dream of nothing else—A jump from finikin beaux to Grave Lawyers!—I do not [think?] the change a bad one—I think _Madame la Presidente_ or Madam _La Conseilleire_ will sound _tres Jolie_.

48 For example, see _A Brief for Her Grace the Duchess of Kingston_ (London: Printed for George Allen, 1776); _The Trial of Elizabeth Duchess Dowager of Kingston for Bigamy_ (London: Printed for Charles Bathurst, 1776); and _The Whole of the Evidence on the Trial of her Grace Elizabeth, Duchess Dowager of Kingston_ (London: Sold by G. Kearsley, 1776).

Instead of politics and the law, Anna channeled her energies into her family, her role as unofficial censor, and her private journals. Those journals have begun to receive the scholarly treatment they deserve as rich sources of British literary and cultural history. The Lewis Walpole Library manuscripts discussed here help to enhance their value and our understanding of Anna. One hopes that there are more "yearly books" from her early life yet to be discovered.

Facsimiles
of the Diary *and* Letters

Monday morning 7 O'Clock
April y.e 15th /76

I can absolutely settle to nothing. — No Chaos ever equalled my head at present, & I will venture to pronounce the heads of half y.e People in this great Town. This day the Duchess of Kingston is tried for Bigamy — the whole Town has talked of nothing else, for this week past. — We are particularly fortunate for without any applications, we have an overflow of Tickets two every day whilst it lasts in the Gallery, belonging to y.e Board of Works, & this day I go with Lady Bathurst in y.e Lord High Steward Box which holds but 36 persons — Miss Atwood goes with her tomorrow. — My Father & Brother go this day with the Board of Work Tickets — & George tomorrow has y.e supreme felicity of going as one of the Lord H: Stewards 20 Gentlemen Attendants, who go through the whole day near him, & hear y.e Debates in the House of Lords. — I up since 5 O'Clock — attending my Hairdresser 'tho we do not leave this house this half hour. I shall give you a more ample History of y.e whole as I go through with it every day Wednesday Morning   the summer

1R

[36]

Wednesday Morning. — Soon after I ended on monday the summons to depart arrived. — I was to meet Lady Bathurst at a Coffee House adjoining ye House of Lords where she has taken a Room while ye Tryal lasts — here her company (who had tickets for her Box) assembled a Breakfast was prepared &c, but I amused myself in seeing the Peers & Peeresses coming into ye Hall from their Carriages, wch were mostly elegant ones, & ye Horses full harness'd & ornamented. — Every thing was orderly & quiet in Palace Yard, ye Guards were very diligent & drawn up under arms. — wch was a pretty sight. — At about ten we all went into the Hall, & took our places in the High Stewards Box, the first Coup d'Œil of ye Hall filled with well dressed people was extreamly striking, ye Peers were scattered about, & we waited an hour before ye Procession came in You must wait much longer for I'm obliged to end so adieu ——————

1ʀ

Thursday Noon. — You must suppose yourself with me in ye Hall, at about eleven on Monday enter'd the procession, in the following order — 1st The Lord High Steward's attendants consisting of 20 gentlemen walking two & two; nor was it an unpleasing sight to see a number of these who were pretty, genteel, well dress'd young men walking round, stoping opposite the Throne, to wch each made his Bow as he pass'd. — after them came as still handsomer set, Peers eldest Sons, & Peers minors unrobed: these were mostly Lads, some among them charming Boys. — then came ye Clerks of ye Council. — after them came ye Masters in Chancery two & two in their Gowns & Bands. — then ye Judges in ye same order in their scarlet robes & caps. — the Bishops next, whose robes are very ungraceful, & being mostly old men I cannot say I was charmed by any of their Lordships — the two Archbishops closed ye Spiritual Tribe, walking with their trains borne, & after paying obeisance to the Throne they took their places on ye side of Benches — the Peers follow'd, commencing with the junior Baron: the Barons are distinguished by having but two rows of ermine on ye right arm of their robes; the Earls who followed them have 3 — the Dukes 4. — When all reached ye Throne, ye Gentlemen Deputy Gentleman marshaled them out, according to their seniority & so took their seats, commencing with the youngest Baron — After ye Dukes, came ye Duke of Cumberland, who as Prince of ye Blood walked alone, with his train borne. — then came Heralds

Herald
2 poursuivants at Arms in their dresses of Ceremony, on
wᶜʰ are quartered the Arms of England &c — they were follow'd
by 4 Serjants at Arms, only distinguished by their Collars, & yᵉ Maces they
bear. Garter King at Arms was next in his strange dress more
like yᵉ Heralds Poursuivants only still more on it. — The Usher of yᵉ Black
Rod Sir Francis Molyneux tres bien poudrée tres bien habillé
marched after him. — the Secretary of yᵉ Briefs — & I think yᵉ
Purse bearer preceded the Lord High Steward, who walked
in his Robes, his Train borne & only marked by a large
black Hat like a Quaker's. & his Staff of office a long white
ward — this closed yᵉ Procession. — the Attendant & Peers soon
ranged themselves on each side, under yᵉ Throne, yᵉ Canopy, & within yᵉ
Throne. — the Bishops & Peers took their seats. — the Chancery masters in their
& The Judges — The Lord H. Steward sat on yᵉ Woolpack nearest yᵉ Throne

1v

The Clerks of the K^s Bench & Council were already seated at ye Table — ye Herald — Garter King at Arms — ye Black Rod stood behind ye Lord High Steward. — till ye ceremony began — the Council for ye two sides had taken their places before ye procession entered. to give you a clearer idea of ye procession & ye arrangement, I have drawn a pretty exact (tho very rough blotted sketch, of Westminster Hall in its present state, & I refer you to that. ye dots are meant to shew ye manner in wch ye Procession walked, & ye figures that the place where they stopped to Bow. —

    The Procession enter'd — the Peers seated — Silence was proclaim'd by the Herald — The Clerks of the Council read ye Kings Commission to The Lord High Steward, the Cause, & reason of its ~~especial endorsement~~ again Then Garter King at Arms introduced ye Usher of ye Black Rod, who with three reverences on his Knee deliver'd the Lord High Steward a long white wand as ye badge of his office. — upon wch He rose from ye wool-pack & walk'd to a Seat on ye last step of ye Throne — The Herald then call'd ye Prisoner into the Court — "This is call'd "Yourself Duchess Dowager of Kingston stand to you "& come into ye Court!" is ye manner he call'd Then Entered ye renowned Duchess within the Bar by 2 Ladies; handed in by ~~her~~ her Bail M^r La Roch by her second Bail Lord Mount Stewart — her Chaplain Dr Warren besides. — her train borne — her dress was suitable to the occasion. all Black: — a Black Silk neglige on not a large Hoop — Black Crape Ruffles, not a speck of white discerned — her hair dressed, & a long Black hood most becomingly put on — it came down in a point before to her forehead, & being wired out, & falling on her shoulders was exactly ye headdress of Mary Queen of Scots in ye old Pictures — Black Gloves & Fan — I have described ye outward appearance — dwell on that 'tile I can resume ye Pen

Tuesday ye 23^d — Now my dear Gertrude I can write without interruption, I will continue my account — I was describing the Dutchesses outward appearance — her aspect was uncon- cerned, seemingly unaffectedly so — she really looked handsome the Lady who attended her was in black & she had three

2R

Chambermaids in White very neatly dressed — That day she read an answer to her inditement — the Attorney general opened the cause — her Council pleaded y^e Sentence of y^e Ecclesiastical Court — the proceedings were tedious & dully delivered. the Court adjourned to the following day = the next day /Tuesday/ the Attorney, & Solicitor General, Mr Dunning & Dr Harris, /Council for y^e prosecution/ were to reply after y^e ~~Lord~~ Procession entered, y^e Lord High Steward, the Lords taken their places, every thing passed as before as to forms, & a most entertaining reply occupy'd us for some time on y^e whole, the Lords adjourned to their house to debate, on their return the Dutchess Council desiring ~~leave~~ time to reply the Court adjourned to Friday = On that day Wallace /her Council/ reply'd; Mr Thurloe drew up y^e Evidence in a most masterly manner — One Witness to prove y^e marriage was examined = Saturday I did not attend, nei- ther did, Witnesses were examined for the Prose-

Monday I attended — Witnesses were examined her every one of whom proved more for y^e Pro- ran any who appeared against the Duchess; — her defence; — the Lords debated in their Hous return each Lord gave his opinion in the follow manner. ye Lord High Steward sitting on ye Throne — the King at Arms with the list of ye Peerage on one side

2v

side, ye Usher of ye Black Rod on ye other - beginning with ye minor Baron said John ~~Baron~~ Lord Sundridge what says ye Lordship? is ye Prisoner guilty or not guilty of ye Felony whereof She stands indited?" He answered standing up uncovered - "Guilty upon my honor" laying his hand upon his breast. thus every Lord delivers his opinion being called upon by name - the Lord High Steward gave his law, every one pronounced her Guilty excepting the Duke of Newcastle who in consideration of his friendship for ye late Duke said he believed her erroneously, not intentionally guilty. then the Lord High Steward had the prisoner called to the Bar & told her She was found guilty. She recd ye sentence with composure. ~~She~~ I suppose she heard her fate before, but She was unable to speak

2ly She wrote on a scrap of paper that she pleaded ye priviledge of peerage, according to the statutes: upon that the Attorney General rose to prove ye invalidity of her plea; ~~too~~ by quoting divers statutes — her second council ~~Dr~~ (Mansfield) answered him, the Lords went to their house to debate. on their return the Lord High Steward on the Throne spoke nearly to this effect — "Madam. the Lords have considered your plea, & admit it; but should you ever be guilty of ~~ye like offence~~ (felony again) it "will be deemed Capital. — at present I discharge you with "no other punishment than the stings of your own Consciencia "& that is punishment sufficient, on such crimes! You "are to be discharged on paying your fees" (which by ye bye they say will be immense) —— This sentence most awefully delivered made an impression on every one, the unhappy woman who rec.d it even seemed sensibly touched — After that Sir S. Molyneux on his knee delivered the rod to the Lord H⟨igh⟩ St⟨eward⟩ who on his entrance into the Court had given it to h⟨im⟩ ⟨then⟩ the proclaimation was made for disso⟨lving⟩ ⟨th⟩ Steward said — "Thus ⟨I disso⟩ve my commission." & he broke his ⟨staff⟩

& Thus ended this trial, of w.ch I here ⟨give a⟩ sketch, but as I was particularly atten⟨tive to the⟩ whole, ~~you~~ I shall draw up an account ⟨of ye⟩ ⟨p⟩roceedings, which I will send you, tho' I mak⟨e⟩ ⟨no doubt ye⟩ trial will be published, how ever ⟨if⟩ ⟨... most pleasing⟩

3ʀ

no doubt ... trial & will be your ...,
production of a female Pen may be most pleasing
to a Female reader —

I should have told you that The Duchess had a most
horrid fit ye last day, wch made a sad hub bub in
ye Hall; I never saw any thing more shocking, she
was carry'd out, & ye proceeding stopped for half an hour
I must beg you will return my paper of ye proceedings
for I am so lazy I cannot copy it, & I should wish to
have it to help my memory. —— Yours Ever
                                        Anna M Porter

3r

P. S. A month ago I raved about chapeaux plumées

& fine Men, I now am in love with nothing but long

wigs, gowns, & Bands; as to Mr Thurloe ye Attorney general,

I think or dream of nothing else — A jump from

finikin beaux to grave Lawyers! I do not the think

the change, a bad one — I think Madame la Presidente or Mada

la Conseilleire will sound tres Jolie —

Do you know Thurloe? he has such a tongue! & such

sensible Eyes! that he may plead any cause even to a

Lady. — but I am a mere rattle just now. Adieu

Oh I must tell you! Madame Adingdon was in our

Box ye first day — little taken notice of, & very disagreeable

giving herself a thousand airs she was not ye least acquaint

ed with me, & I did not think it worth my while to b

go with her — She was asleep, tired, asked Lad y — to go away

Who gave her a short answer, to say she

made her look very fo

good set downs, & took

was out of patience with the nonsense

made her observations on Mr Wallace in

tinent manner, to the Speaker with whom

acquainted, he at last as civilly as he

her to hold her tongue for Mrs Wallace s

& he could bear it no longer — Another fool

that I believe ye good Lady wished herself away — I wished

3v

[46]

her so — Leathly — her Sister in Law was coming but fell down & sprained her ancle — Adieu again.

The Husband was there the second day looking as Cross as a Devil & as discontented à l'ordinaire

Wednesday Morning — I was at Rovières Ball last night Madame Abingdon there & knew me — spoke. — & Guess who was there besides The Sweet Squire — her neither ~~neither~~ knew nor spoke to me — at which I was glad — Miss R — said he looked like a Journeyman Grocer dressed out for y.e occasion could I after that wish for his conversation. — She would not take away the Sweet from him so called him
                                                                    a Grocery Merchant

3v

A shorte account of the Proceedings on the trial of the Duchess
Dowager of Kingston for bigamy before the Lord High Steward &
her Peers in Westminster Hall — Commenced on ye 15th of April
1776

After the first ceremonials, such as reading ye Commission granted to
the Lord High Steward &c — the Prisoner's indictement was read to this
effect, that she Elizabeth Chudleigh after marrying Mr Hervey, marry'd
the Duke of Kingston during the Life of her first Husband. When she
appear'd, the Lord High Steward in a short speech told her the crime for
which she was indicted, dwelt on the heinousness of it, on the consequences arising to society from such examples; in a word he opened
the Commission in a solemn, aweful, manner. — She reply'd to
her indictement by a short speech, wherein she complain'd of the
cruelty of her prosecutors; declared her sense of the justice & equity
that would guide her Judges; & her hopes of having her innocence appear. — this she delivered with composure, & apparent fortitude. —
Then the Attorney General (Mr Thurloe) clearly stated the Reasons
of the prosecution, adding that a cause of Jactitation was instituted in the Ecclesiastical Court by Miss Chudleigh against Mr Hervey
& a sentence obtained in that Court by which the marriage was
not properly annulled but rather deny'd, not admitted; A Cause of
Jactitation he explain'd as follows; that on a Man's boasting or
publickly declaring that such a Woman is his Wife, she is authorized to commence a suit in Docter's Commons against him, calling
on him to prove her his Wife, or retract his claim then that
Court gives sentence according to the proofs. he intimated that
the Sentence procur'd by the Prisoner was obtained by Collusion
but

supposing Her Council would notwithstanding insist on its being in force as a prevention of the Trial, he desired it might be read to the Lords. — Lord Mansfield rose & opposed this request, alledging that reading the sentence would lead to farther examinations into the allegations for & against the marriage, that the Evidences given into ye Ecclesiastical Court must be produced, in a word besides the loss of time the whole would be of no use. — Thurloe in his reply maintained, & gain'd his ground. — The several proceedings in the Ecclesiastical Court were read, as well as the Sentence. these had pass'd (I think) during 3 or 4 different years, & were introductory to the pleadings of the Council on both sides. — Mr Wallace first Council for the Prisoner open'd the Cause. he began by farther explaining ye meaning of a cause of Jachtation, his aim being to prevent a trial, & to turn the whole on ~~an~~ points of Law, whether or not any Court whatsoever could properly be appeal'd to against a Sentence given in the Ecclesiastical Court, whether whilst that sentence was in force any Court could proceed in examinations; & whether supposing those examinations are made any Court has ye power of repealing the Sentence? — innumerable were the arguments he advanced to prove that these were impossible; unprecedented; Cases were brought in, to shew that they were unprecedented. — To the charge against the sentence of its being procured by Collusion not having ground for denying it, he indirectly admitted it, stated many cases in wch Sentences so obtained had taken place, had been rec^d by other Courts, he dwelt always on the Sentence & its force, avoiding as much as possible entering into a regular discussion of the means by wch it was obtained — Mr Wallace is universally admired & give

you

4v

an account of how things appear'd to me, rather than how they
are; I must therefore say that to the eye of mere common Sense
& observation, he seemed to make the most of a bad cause:
his manner is unpleasing, & 'tho his language may be good
it seems inelegant from the badness of the delivery, from
a heat & vehemence in his manner that rather fatigues
than strikes the hearers. — Mr Mansfield the Prisoner's
second Council, took up Mr Wallaces pleadings when he
ended. — A number of new Cases wch he produced some from
Viner's abridgements some from Sir John Strange's reports (wch
latter had been likewise quoted by Wallaces) these innumerable instances rather served to confuse the memory of his
audience, than give light to the Cause; the ground work of his speech) was the same as the
preceding Councils, the inferences drawn from it seemed to
be different from his rather in words than in Matter. —
Two Civilians Dr Calvert & Dr Winn (both retained for the
Prisoner) continued the pleadings in her favour. the Contrast
between these was striking, the first joined to a drawling
voice a length of periods & a dullness of Composition that
operated mostly as opiates on those who attended. the other
by a spirited manner, & lively turn of expression rouzed them
for a while, 'tho the sameness of the subject rendered his efforts of transient use. — They chiefly spoke in favor of their
Court gave new lights into its forms of proceeding, but
both they & Mansfield admitted the Collusion in the Dutchess
obtaining the Sentence. — After keeping the Court very long
on these points it adjourned to the following day when the
Council for the Prosecution were to reply. —

5R

I should have mention'd that each Council founded the impossibility of bringing on the trial, on a Statute of Henry ye 8th by wch all sentences given by the Ecclesiastical Court were deemed final & decisive in all cases whatsoever; this was a great road to all ye Law of the land; very edifying to those who understood it but you will not be surprized when I say I was not able to retain enough to repeat it intelligibly to you.

Tuesday the 16th was the second day of the Trial — The Attorney General (Mr Thurloe) enter'd on the reply. — His manner, voice, address command attention: His strength of reasoning, justness of argument, propriety of Language, demand applause; & to judge of others by myself highly bespeak partiality. — He began by examining the manner in which the Sentence so vehemently urged had been obtained; then this naturally lead into a general survey of ye usual method of giving sentences in that Court. — He concluded from the first, that no sentence or suit of wch fraud & deception had been ye guides cd hold — from the second he made others conclude the Court he described a very villainous one. — in the course of what he said on that head he, in the following ludicrous manner gave this account "How are Sentences given? thus. the Court assembled, "the Judges & Docters setting round the Table, the one, who preside "gives an example wch ye rest follow or perhaps have already "given, he falls asleep — maybe grows hungry, or tired, or any "thing. — "Come, come (cries he) let's dispatch business; come "let's give Sentence!" — Every one is unanimous to dispatch "business, to give Sentence, but how depends on ye momentary "whim or resolve — however (added Thurloe looking round "most expressively) Sentence is given. & that Sentence You "my Lords are desired & expected to abide by."

2.º) he answer'd very ably the several pleas of of the Prisoner's Council; & prefaced his answers by saying that he should have been asham'd to have appear'd with such pleas in favour of a Client. for by dwelling on a Sentence w.ch they indirectly tho clearly granted was procured by fraud, refusing to have it examined into, & 2.º Cause tried, either employ'd their sense of the guilt of their Client; or their judging the Tribunal before w.ch she was called incapable of deciding — He threw aside the mere Sentence & highly inveighed against the means by which it was obtained — he endeavour'd to deduce all his arguments against the Prisoner, from those brought in for her viewed in another light. and even turned the Cases urged as precedents, &c, into the same Channel. — their Plea of the Statute of Henry y.e 8.th & the string of Law following it he repaid by opposite statutes, & by Law — I own here all his abilities could not gloss over y.e force of that statute, for those he mentioned as contradictory to it required the help of supposition to assist one in finding them such, & rather must ~~by either~~ ~~or the like~~ be made to mean what he concluded they did mean — however be cautious of what I say on this subject, for I always remind you that I represent things as they appear'd to my capacity. — what he aim'd at was to bring on the trial. — to sum up the whole, all he advanced was to the point in question; all he remarked was to the purpose of that point.

M.r Wedderburne as Solicitor General continued the subject on the Crown side. — the text being still the same, variety could not be expected; the wish of procuring it however, exerted the abilities of this able Lawyer — he ran over what Thurloe had urged; he answered some cases

the other had omitted, he gave several to the point wch acquired
double merit from his manner of stating them; he was still more
poignant on the Ecclesiastical Court, & raised many laughs at its expence: Thurloe upon the whole enterd into a solemn exposition
of its errors & villainies; Wedderburne into a ludicrous one —
In one part of his speech he gave a detail of the case with
wch Sentences to annull one marriage, & confirm another, or to do
either seperately are obtaind -- then he continued nearly to this
effect --- "Should your Lordships sanction be given to these sentences
"by declaring ye impossibility of an appeal from the Court, ex-
"peditions to ye Fleet will considerably diminish, the Journey
"thither be considerably shortened, parties may stop at St Pauls where
"they will find the indulgent Doctors kindly ready to accommo-
"date matters according to the directions given them"
In another part he said — "So easily, so expeditiously, so pleasan-
"-ly are matters carryd on there, that it has been found on a very
"moderate computation that a Man who is fond of Polygamy
"may from ye age of 21 to that of 35 have 75 wives — Now for
"heavens sake My Lords whatever you do in your private
"character do not encourage Poligamy in your judicial ones"
Nor was he contented with striking at their conduct in similar cases to that before the Court, he endeavourd to expose it
in others stating the following case was a Coup de main as it hit ye
opposite Council a severe blow ---
"A Case was brought into Court" (whether of Common Pleas,
Kings bench, or Exchequer I do not recollect) "as follows. — A Man
"had forged a Will as if made by a Woman who at the time
"he forged it he declared Dead in Jamaica — he obtained a Probit
of

6v

"the Will in Docters Commons — he took possession of Money she had
"in the funds in consequence; for by the will that money was be-
"queathed to him. — The heir at Law, or some person concerned
"offered to prove the will was false, was forged, brought a suit in
"court by which he litigated it. — What evidence did he produce
"to prove these assertions? the Woman herself whose will it was
"supposed to be. She declared that she never had been dead, never
"had made a will, was then alive in Court as they saw. — could
"any thing be more absurd than to demur on such proof? did
"a doubt arise? — according to the Gentlemen on the other side
"the Bar there could. they say no Sentence given in that Court
"can be repealed, they declare it infallible — in this instance
"the Probit was full & clear, the decision evident. what must
"we conclude my Lords? that Woman was dead to all intends &
"purposes? for — She was dead in Law " — He advanced but
little concerning ye Statute, throwing his opinion into what Thus-
loe had said on the Subject — he even ventured an abuse of Strange
reports saying they were carelessly, incautiously compiled in
a word he appeared as able as a Man could appear, after Thurma
He Weddersburne has not his advantages of Voice — You see him exert
himself whereas ye other seems secure by having reflected on his
point, & maintains an uniform constant superiority which that
Reflection seems to inspire. — He endeavours to convince by
urging one to make use of ones own Common Sense & shews
what that hint — Weddersburne's Manner appears to say I will
convince you — they severally succeed, 'tho the former in the
most pleasing manner. — Perhaps had I heard Wedderburne first
I should have been more struck with his uncommon Powers
a tired attention is a real disadvantage 'tho mine was very
little so. — I never heard more real humour than he possesses

he makes every one laugh but himself, & seems surprized
that they laugh, whilst ye surprize may be returned that he can
keep up his dry gravity. — Who could enter ye lists after these
Oratours? — Dunning did — 'tho doubtless ill fitted for it — to an
exceeding bad person is joined the false conviction of being perfectly
handsome. imagine ye ridiculous composition this forms! — imagine
that composition appearing at a grave & solemn Bar! — & thence
conclude that imagination cannot design a more ridiculous
object. — a voice nearly abstract accompany'd with a
constant, hollow, Cough. — at the end of every period comes a
Cough — at ye beginning a hem — Oh! the agreeable Oratour. —
But let us leave manners, & dwell on the matter it so ill expressed. — Here I own myself no judge; a great deal of Law; a great
deal of quibbling on words; a number of Cases from Chapter
this, & page "that" as "your Lordships may see"; added to some
personal wit on ye prisoner; I found out "there is the quantity
as for the quality I could not distinguish its worth, my own
ignorance perhaps, occasion'd this mental near sightedness. —
You will wonder at this for Dunning is esteem'd uncommonly
clever. — I answer you by two proverbs — "Habit is second nature"
those who admire him are habituated to his manner, & pass
that over. — "Comparaisons are odious" I compared him to
Thurloe & Wedderburne which would never hold. — Law is not
food for every one, & must be well dress'd & well seasoned to
be palatable, a quantity surfeits one at once. — the Person-
ality I complained of in Dunning, was his saying that if sentences
in ye Ecclesiastical court were rendered so infallible, people
might marry & unmarry as they pleased, & even the Earl of Bristol lay claim to the Lady at the Bar 'tho he added "'tis not very likely
"he should." what use for this sarcasm?

3.) Dunning's harangue was divided into so many parts second, third, fourth, & so on, — contained so many "to concludes" that I thought it never would end — I was ready to faint when I saw another black robed Gentleman rise to continue ye reply; however, I found my disapprobation of Dunning proceeded not from fatigue, as Dr Harris's want of voice did not prevent my attending to & being pleased with, his speech. — He is a Civilian & has a respectable aspect — 'tho his voice is low, indistinct, unpleasing, yet his manner is good & he has a propriety of action that attaches one's attention. — he began so modestly that I forgot he was the 4th Lawyer who had occupy'd the Court. — he said that after hearing the subject so uncommonly well handled, it was presumption in him to trouble ye Court any longer, for he could have nothing to add: that as to Cases it appeared to him unnecessary to cite any to prove what simple common sense ^sufficiently proved therefore all he should say would be to give them an incite into the forms of this Court, & shew them how far they might proceed in the appeal now before them. — this he did very concisely & well. I left the Hall after this harangue — the Lords adjourned to their House to debate on ye steps to be taken for or against the Sentence — on their return to the Hall Lord Talbot moved for an adjournment of ye Court — Wallace was asked if he purposed a reply ^on his side & he answer'd that he did & desired time to draw it up in — it was granted him, & notwithstanding an effort was made to conclude it that day, ye Court was adjourned untill Friday ye 19th

8 R

[57]

Friday the 19th — The proceedings began by Mr Wallaces reply
he had a bad cause; he had sifted every word to be urged for his
side before; what could he do? why no otherwise than he did
cast away as much as possible ye material pointed arguments
& dwell on trifles wch he twisted about as well as he could;
give us case upon case to lead us from ye consequential objection
first he carryd us on board ship into the West Indies with a Sailor
whose wages had been embezzled; then he tripped from turnpike Roads to cross Lanes & brought cases from the conduct of
Commissioners of Highways, Carts, & Waggons; — he wished to entertain us
by his witticisms, what effect they had on others I cannot determine
as for me whilst I was finding out in what ye first Joke consisted a second came, & then a third like Banquo's race shewn as
Kings to Macbeth: I might say with him "Another & another, &
"another, & still ye last bears semblance to the first - & mark
"another yet." — You saw a Man piqued, vexed; it was impossible to biass one effectually by means of reason against this
Cause his antagonists so ably pleaded he wished therefore by Personal
reflexions on the opposite Council to turn us against the Men not
the Cause they handled. — he thus answer'd Thurloe's description of
the Judges of ye Ecclesiastic court & ye manner in wch they give
Sentences. — "I have no doubt some time hence to see my
"learned friend raised by his uncommon abilities to the first Law
"posts in this Kingdom, then I hope it will never be reproach'd
"him . that he left a Cause undecided from indolence. or
"because his friend expected him at Table; or that for ye sake
"of future repose he submitted to present dispatch of business"
Nothing could be harsher than this sarcasm; nothing more
ungenerous; for Thurloe is remarkable for his extreme Laziness
& his indolence has been his only fault in business — I wish it had
been his only one in through his moral conduct through life. —

to Dunning who had spoken contemptuously of Viner's abridgment
Wallace said "recollect that most of y.e wealth he now possesses he
"owes to Viner. — & most of y.e Law your Lordships have paid for &
"do pay for is f.t out of Viner." — in a word Wallace neither
gained himself or his cause credit by his reply. — I think D.r
Calvert continued it; & Thurloe answer'd him by a short speech
but here my attention dropp'd. — I follow'd the example for
y.e moment of some Noble Lords — I must mention one who
when first y.e Court met rose in a mumble, mumble, & after
talking (half an hour) for his own edification I suppose, as I am sure nobody
else heard him / at last by raising his voice he told us that
he moved that / the Lords should examine the Sentence given in
the Ecclesiastical Court, & determine whether or not a trial
could be proceeded on. — imagine how every one stared for
what else had they been about since their meeting? however
notwithstanding / y.e general laugh, & call to order Lord Mansfield rose., & by his able speech made us forget or rather
forgive the blundering Lord — he answer'd & told him that he
must either have been remiss in his attendance, attention
or enquiries not to know that that had been their busyness for three days
he afterwards in y.e easiest, clearest, manner, ran over
y.e several proceedings for his information; & to help y.e
general recollection of y.e Court. — After Wallace's speech Lord
Carlisle asked him some very pertinent questions, & y.e degree
of modesty & diffidence with w.ch he put them, added not a
little to their merit — So true it is that y.e world is ever ready
to give praise where not demanded by & a confident self
sufficiency. —

9 R

After the reply the Lords adjourned to their own house, to ask y.e opinion of y.e Judges, ~~opinion~~ & debate on y.e Justness of bringing on the trial — we waited for them some time during w.ch I learnt from my brother (who attended in y.e House) that the Lord High Steward asked y.e Judges whether they thought the trial according to Law? the Chief Justice De Grey answer'd in the name of His brethren that they were unanimously for the trial — he said his speech was one of y.e Noblest pieces of Oratory ever heard. So much Eloquence, so much Law, so much universal learning, — such Good language, & such manners. — after debates y.e Lords return'd. — The Lord High Steward told the Attorney General to proceed in the Prosecution. Then Thurloe shone in setting forth the Evidence — he began by awefully enumerating the ill consequences of such crimes to moral order, civil society & religion — to the Laws of God & Man. — after dwelling some time on those considerations, after enforcing them by forcible similes & Oratorical figures — he shew'd the various circumstances that ~~aggravated~~ this particular commission of the crime, the Collusion that follow'd it, the perjury that accomplished it — as a stronger shade to this picture he stated all that could be in general urged as excuses to such faults, & then proved that none of them could be alledged in excuse of this error. — "It was not y.e heat "of intemperate Youth; the force of blind Passion; that led the "Parties on — 'twas Dry Lucre suggested it & Cold Fraud perpetrated "it." — — Then again he added — "Nay it clearer appears that "the Lady was perfectly indifferent which Husband remained "hers. provided She had the richest, & y.e one who gave her y.e "highest Rank." — — After these general observations he entered into an account of y.e Evidence he should bring in; w.ch in fact was a history of the renowned Dutchess to the following effect. —

4th) The Lady at the Bar is born of a reputable, of an honourable Gentleman's family; ye younger branch of a Baronet's family: She was educated in the paths of virtue; She was led by the guidance of Prudence & Discretion, too soon She forfeited all pretensions to the precepts these teach. — She was recd into the Princess Dowager of Wales's family as her Maid of Honour, & for some time supported the character she bore when first She entered that service. — I am uncertain if Mr Thurloe said that She was maid of Honour before or after her marriage with Mr Harvey. — About August (I think 54 but dates I really forget) She went down into Hampshire on a Visit to a Mr Merylls at Lanestown in Hamps during with her Aunt Mrs Hanmore; during her stay there She accompanyd Her Aunt & ye family they were with, to Winchester Races there She became acquainted with Mr Harvey — their acquaintance was soon ripen'd into an intimacy — The reasons of so speedy a connection we will attribute to advances from the Lady wch were perhaps solicited, if not they were readily answered by the Gentleman. Whether he continued in the neighbourhood only, or came immediately to Mr Merylls house, I do not recollect but I think the former — after a short time a marriage was agreed on by the Parties — Reasons of Prudence on both sides occasiond their resolving it should be a Clandestine one. those on Mr Harvey's part proceeded from ye fear of ye Earl of Bristols disapprobation, & ye impossibility of his succeeding in the World without the patronage of such a relation. — Miss Chudleigh's Establishment in life, her being already in the Princesses family, or hoping to be so (points I do not exactly remember) made her readily agree to ye privacy of ye Marriage. Mr Merylls house was situated in the parish of Lanerton there was no other house in the Parish or rather no house of any consideration — The Church was at the end of his garden & door open'd from thence into the Church Yard. — At Eleven O'Clock, at night in the month of August. Mr Harvey & Miss Chudleigh accompany'd by Mr Sheryle, Mrs Hanmore, a Mr ~~Bourn~~ Montevas ~~& Poultney~~ ~~& some such name~~ ~~went to the Church where~~ & Anne Craddock Mrs Hanmore's Maid! Mr Ames ~~& one~~ ~~& Hainor~~ y Clergyman of that Parish marry'd them. — I believe the very next day Mr Harvey left Laneston & went to join y Fleet at ~~Plymouth~~ Portsmouth ~~which~~ was then under y Command of Sr John Davers. — destined I think for y West Indies. I believe it was two years before he returned, during wch time she had a house in Conduit Street where she recd him, where several of their friends saw them; & where they lived & were regarded as Man & Wife. — She likewise had one child there. If I remember right he made a second voyage, & it was not this 5 y that a disgust & disagreement arose between them. upon what account the Attorney General intimated only. — however they determined to part — He sent her several messages to propose a Divorce; offered several methods; at length he wanted her to declare that she was Criminal in her Conduct, in order to forward y proceeding in case he commenced a suit. — She sent him an answer of y most indelicate cast declaring She would not. — Upon the Earl of Bristols being dangerously ill & declared Dying (tho he afterwards recover'd.) — She went Post down to Winchester, to y Clergyman who had marry'd her, & who had a Parish in Winchester, or was retired there. She put up at an Inn opposite to his House. — The particulars of y visit she made him were minutely related, She desired him to give her a Certificate of her Marriage ~~& a Copy of y Register~~ to that purpose ~~She had brought~~ ~~down with her stampt paper (a particular paper used in those~~ case)

~~unfortunately the poor Parson knew not how to execute, I would not, till he had seen Mrs Merylle or some other person who could direct him in the use of it, & shew him the manner of~~ but could not in ye manner of giving it, however

Mr Meryll was sent for, set them right, & she obtained her a rezister of her marriage a rezister book being bought & ye ~~certificate &c.~~ — The Earl of Bristol recover'd; the Certificate & Rezister were forgotten; Ld Bristol's heir sunk into Mr Hervey & her Husband, She entered afresh into his schemes for dissolving the marriage — thus the Attorney General proved wt he first advanced that She valued the Husband according to his riches, & ye rank he gave her. — She was then as anxious to be Lady Bristol, as she since has shew'd herself to be Duchess of Kingston — Her first connexion with ye Duke of Kingston the public manner in wch she lived with him, are generally known, during that time Hervey justly accused her of criminality, but whether the want of proofs, or ye power of money, or other reasons prevented him, he did not attempt a Divorce tho he talked of, & wished it. — At length an expedient was found She was to bring in a suit of Jactitation against him, he was to acquiesce in it, the accommodating Doctors of ye Ecclesiastical Court building on ye ~~Statute~~, actuated by ye love of power & of Gain, drew up a form of Oaths; were dictated in the steps they took; ~~doctors~~ formed a Sentence — in a word Doctered up as pretty a dose of roguery fraud, & villainy, as ever stood on ye record of ye most infamous Crew of Civil, Ecclesiastical, or no order of Men. — soon after this on ye sufficiency of this Sentence Miss Chidleigh marry'd the D. of Kingston a credulous, weak Man. — depending solely on ye declaration of ye Ecclesiastical Court, whereby she was declared a Spinster. — — I have here repeated from

11r

mere memory the head of y.ᵉ Attorney General's speech, you
must allow / for mere memory ⸺ I wish I could have
given you his Language; his observations, his similes;
he summ'd up this narrative by saying that the witnesses
he had to bring in would prove all he advanced. ⸺ That he
moreover had the Register of her marriage to produce; ~~with~~

~~his hands in the following extraordinary manner, the Parish of~~
~~Lanreston after the marriage was united to that of Sand-~~
~~croft, Crancroft, or some croft, I do not remember~~
~~the Clergyman of this neighbouring Parish officiated at Lanreston~~
~~sometimes, oftener, y.ᵉ parishioners went to Sandcroft~~
~~best to Church — there was no person of any consideration~~
~~in Lanreston but Mr Meryll, the Register book therefore~~
~~was kept at his House, there being no resident clergyman~~
~~it found inconvenient to have it out of the Parish~~
~~Mr Meryll died, & was succeeded in his House, Estates,~~
~~&c by a distant relation who of course had y.ᵉ Register~~
~~book in his hands, tho perhaps he had not y.ᵉ heart, far~~
~~having it, that Meryll had, who was in Miss Chudleigh's~~
~~secret — the register now is in that Gentleman's possession~~
~~& might be produced~~

The Solicitor General was then directed to examine the Witnesses
on y.ᵉ Crown side. — the first who was sworn was Anne
Craddock ⁓ Mrs Hanmore's maid y.ᵉ only surviving witness
of y.ᵉ former Marriage. ⸺ Her Evidence was very clear. ⸺
She was present at y.ᵉ marriage, she was employ'd to
keep y.ᵉ other servants away, /from it/ She heard the Ceremony w.ᶜʰ
was perform'd by /y.ᵉ light of/ a Taper stuck in Mr Montagu's Hat
She told us many other particulars; said that the Prisoner

11v

5th) offer'd to cor her to see her Child; that she carry'd her messages between her & Harvey concerning the Divorce. in short many circumstances were repeated proving her thorough knowledge of ye fact — one thing she did not so clearly answer to, whether or not she had any promise of emolument from ye Prosecutors if her Evidence accused ye prisoner — it was some time before they got a flat answer on the negative; indeed the poor woman was so questioned that I wonder she could say any thing such cross & re cross Examination!

It grew so late that there was no possibility of concluding this examination; the Court was adjourned to the next day Saturday ye 20th —

Saturday ye 20th I did not attend; but my Brother did, I can therefore repeat from him what passed in order to cor on ye Thread of ye Tale — My nonattendance proceeded from my imagining ye Evidences would be rather unfit for a Female Ear. — I was disappointed, for I suppose no trial of such a stamp was carry'd on with ye Delicate Decency this was.

Anne Craddocks examination continued & ended during wch several Lords asked questions, the Duke of Grafton many, & really some his Grace might have omitted if not most. — one was particularly laugh'd at. how many servants there were in Mrs Meryll's family? the poor Old woman began & gave us a detail of every Cat & dog in ye family; Birth, Parentage, & Education. Lord Effingham talked we would have pardoned that, but Alas! he would be heard too. — the Duke of Richmond finding Superlative pleasure in the sound of his own voice bellow'd out

much

nonsense. — on Saturday after Anne Craddock — Mr Ceasar Hawkins was examined — his Evidence was clear & pointed but
rather a corroborating than a direct one. — he proved that
he had attended the prisoner during her Lying-in, from his
connection with, & friendship for, Harvey. — that afterwards he
carry'd messages from him to her, concerning a divorce, at that
period when Harvey was convinced of her ill conduct but
yet wished for an amicable composition. — Hawkins's behaviour was perfectly honourable; his Evidence perfectly
satisfactory. — Mrs Pettyplace (Lord Howe's Sister) appeared
next, all She declared was that the had always considered the
parties as marry'd; that Miss Chudleigh had told her they were
marry'd. — After this follow'd a strange affair, Lord Barrington
was sworn to "tell y Truth, the whole truth, & nothing but
the truth." he solemnly took the Oath. — After he had taken
it, he hop'd the Court would not expect him to repeat prisoners
Conversations with the Prisoner, for as a Man of honour he
did not think he could. — Every body was amaz'd! this sh'd
have been said before he was sworn. — the Duchess rose &
very generously acquitted him of every consideration, & besought
him to forget her as his friend, & regard her merely as the
then appear'd before y Court. — he persisted in his first
scruple. — it was judged a contempt of the Court, & y Lords
adjourned to their own house, to debate on y punishment
due to such a Contempt. — Lord Camden, Lord Mansfield
spoke to the point, urging that it was a Contempt of their
house but at the same time 'twas not in their power to
take punishable cognizance of it, as y offender was a member

of y.e house of Commons & would have y.e protection of that House. — there were many speeches, many debates: 'till the Lord High Steward rose, & told them that they were mistaken in their conclusion, it was not punishable as a Contempt of a Court of Judicature, but as a Perjury, that private interests were out of y.e question — Conscience was concerned. — I believe this set Lord Barrington right, the Lords return'd to the Hall, & he consulted Thurloe who told him he must declare all he knew. — When he had declared it 'twas merely corroborating, & proved that She had owned her marriage to Harvey. — The most interesting Witness was the next, Anne Philips. She was the Clergyman's wife who marry'd y.e Prisoner at Lanestown, & losing her first Husband She marry'd Phillips the Duke of Kingston's Steward — She proved Miss Chudleighs marriage; proved her coming down to Winchester for y.e Certificate, in a word her Evidence was most satisfactory, & most clear. — I do not recollect hearing of any more Witnesses; the Court adjourned to Monday y.e 22.d — I attended on that day. ————

Monday y.e 22.d — The Lord High Steward asked Thurloe if he had any more witnesses to Examine on the Crown side he said he had not. upon that the Duchess rose to make her defence. it consisted of 13 sheets of Law Paper — not very Coherent, not very Elegant but her situation, the tout ensemble, rendered it interesting. — She began by setting forth her Ancestry. Poor Woman! we all sprang from Adam & perhaps she might particularly be stiled one of Eves Daughters if frailty marked y.e immediate Parentage! She told Us y.e many posts Sir This had fill'd had honourably filled — the many virtuous deeds s.d. That person performd — She told us her last lineal descendant was Sir George Chudleigh her father's ~~elder~~ father. — he was in some battle where he for a considerable time maintained his Post, & defended a Standard 'till at length overcome by numbers he fell; yet resolved never to abandon the English George Colours he stuck it before him, & y.e Colours were shot into his Heart. — She inferrd from the merits of so fair a race that it was natural for her to endeavour to keep up their Virtues in her person; to avoid y.e shame they would feel, were they to think her guilty of such crimes (supposing they as she was accused of could rise from their graves & behold their Kinswoman. from her admission into y.e Princess of Wales's family & continuance therein, she concluded that Princess. mus.t have been convinced of the rectitude of her conduct — allow- ing even that she knew her connection with Harvey, & winked at it, yet surely she could not have approved her marriage with the Duke of Kingston, w.ch not only had her sanction but that of their Majesties who by receiving her at Court shew'd that they thought her not so vile & Nay she said would that great, that worthy, that most virtuous Nobleman y.e Duke of Kingston have united himself to one marked with such crimes. — (Poor Man thought I is this the first time You were called great & time worthy excepting under your painted Arms on y.e road to in y.e Inns Pierpoint above y.e sounding Custos Rotulorum) she entreated y.e Court to consider the interested views that occasi- oned the prosecution against her, which added she might more justly be termd persecution. it was not the Love

13v

6th of virtue; 'twas not ye love of Justice; 'twas black revenge, &
Avarice. — It was not <u>her</u> they meant to punish — her punish-
ment was to be the road to litigating her fortunes, "Was that
"all" (added she) most willingly I would resign them, nothing
"now attaches me to the world, the moment that deprived me
"of ye greatest, best of men, my Loved Lord his Grace of
"Kingston robbed me of all y^t good, I had in this world, all
"I implor'd was death, most patiently I waited for it — had
"not ye duty of self preservation every being owes our
"Almighty God obliged me to use proper means to preserve
"mine — I prize neither Riches nor Titles, any more
"than that the first mark ye confidence my late Lord &
"Husband placed in me — & ye Last is all now remaining
"all now left me as a pledge of a Connection, that formed the
"happiness of my life. — " Oh Woman! Woman! how
Could you utter such untruths! — Much greater Rhapsodies
than these did she spout. She told us that it was the Dukes
will enraged her Ennemies, but She said so far had <del>she</del>
was she, from having
any hand in it, he had unknown to her made 3 wills
at different Periods, were one more favorable to her. —
"encreasing Years encreased his good opinion of her" So
little did she instigate his dissensions with Evelyn Meadows whom he disenherited, that she endeavoured to reconcile them. — that their first quarrel was on Evelyn's
leaving the Army ignobly, & the second his not fulfilling
his engagements with Miss Bishop — She brought up
that old Tale wch harrow'd up my soul. Oh I rejoiced at
all she said against the vile Man for of all those on
whom y^e name of <u>Man</u> is prostituted he is doubtless
vilest

14_R

[69]

vilest & so far ~~from~~ is his mind, from being after y Image of our
Creators – I am sure y Devil has marked him for his
own. – It was in vain for her to contradict her marriage with
Harvey, ~~that~~ She admitted it, but said She thought herself absolved from any connection with him, by y Sentence of y Ecclesiastical Court; that D! Collier of that Court had directed her & y
Duke of Kingston in all they did, that he was present at her
marriage with y Duke; assureing them that they were innocent before
God & Man. D! Collier's health would not permit him to
attend, that She had witnesses to prove he could not attend.
The last part of her defence was purposely lost, She read y
rest but repeated that from memory & shewed her power
in the Pathetic, indeed I never saw a better actress. –
She ended all, by saying 'twas not for life, for riches,
for worldly goods she pleaded, 'twas to beseech them to
defend her honour, her innocence. She laid great stress
on the words that they might be convinced She had not made
a mistake when She took y sacred names in vain. –
Wallace being asked if he had any witnesses to examine for
y Prisoner said he had. but previously desired that Mrs
Phillips might be called in to acknowledge her signature
& handwriting to & in a letter. Anne Phillips was accordingly
called – many Lords rose & said She should not acknowledge her handwriting without the Courts knowing the purport of the letter – this was over ruled She was brought in,
calmly acknowledged her handwriting, read y letter, said it
was hers, & retired. then y letter was read, all it contained
was that She Anne Phillips writ to the Duchess to beg her to
intercede

with the Duke that her Husband might remain in his
service, she was led to this by hearing that ye Duke intended to dismiss him from his Stewardship. — Now in her
Evidence, being asked if her husband left ye Duke of Kingston
from his own choice or ye Dukes will, for supposing it ye
latter malice might have actuated her Evidence — she
answer'd so far from it, that her Husband resigned his
charge under ye Duke of himself. — this letter was brought
to charge her with prevarication. — The Attorney General
rose — he declared it as futile charge for it was very possible ye husband chose to quit ye Duke's service on disagreements, & ye Wife writ this letter unknown to him
hoping to make up matters: indeed ye whole tenor of ye
letter proved the case thus — but as farther proofs he
produced two letters ye first a copy from one of Phillips
in which he makes a full resignation to ye Duke.
the second from ye Duke in his own handwriting accepting the resignation. — After this one Barton Lord
Bristol's Attorney was call'd in. — he looked so like a
Taylor! & made such a snipping Evidence! — he was
call'd in for her, & proved her marriage to Harvey, &
his wanting a Divorce; together with all ye goings
on in the Ecclesiastical Court, more clearly than any witness
against her. — Then Mary Pritchard appeared, as arrant
la femme d'intrigue as ever lived. God forgive her
I am
I sure she was perjured every word she spoke — She
was to prove that Anne Craddock had told her she was
to have an Emolument from ye Meadows's but it

15R

[71]

appeared this woman had been set to worm it out of the
old Creature — Pritchard prevaricated; she first knew a thing
then she forgot it. — She gave no dates, no hint to guess at
dates — Lord Denbigh by very able, pointed questions to her,
proved her too evidently perjured. — She said knew Craddock
told her when she had a fortune & could live independent
she would come & live with her — Mr. Thurlow remarked
that this was very probable (for Pritchard acknowledged herself the
wife of a petty Custom House Officer & that she lived at Mile End)
"It is probable continued he that an independent fortune, riches
"& affluence, should chuse to fix its abode with Mrs Pritchard at
"Mile End — The virtuous wife of a Custom House Porter."
In short poor Mr. Pritchard made a sad figure — during
her evidence there was a sad Hub-bub — the witness stood without ye Bar with the Prisoner, ye Gentleman Usher of ye Black
Rod, & ye Clerk of the Council were between them, ye Duke of
Richmond accused the Prisoner of speaking to the witness — the
Lord H: Steward said there was wrong goings on, & charged
the Court to be more on their guard — I saw all that pass'd
& own I did not perceive her speak, ye Usher was called
out & declared she did not. — My Brother saw the whole
& says she did not speak, but fixed the witness, looking at
her most stedfastly & making her signs. — After Pritchard
Dr. Warren was sworn to prove that Collier was unable
to attend — he declared he could not, without great hazard —
but what species of Hazard whether of Death &C he would
not say — All the complaint he had was St. Anthony's fire,
& it plainly appeared that he was ashamed to come in Court
afraid of having his conduct examined, perhaps punished. —

15v

7th) Then arose a violent debate amongst the Lords in ye Hall – Lord Ravensworth began mumbling, & we found out he wanted Dr Collier examined by interrogatories. – Lord Mansfield answered him briefly, told him it could not be done – previous to that indeed the Lord H. Steward declared it an unprecedented thing, he never had known it done. Lord Ravensworth proceeded however, & persisted in moving it over & over again, 'till he moved every body against him Lord Falconbridge seconded him most vehemently. – Lord Camden answer'd them most calmly & most forcibly – He ran over the different Laws relative to taking Evidences; the ill consequences of interrogatories; the unprecedentedness of them; the impossibility of them: After the most able, ye most Elegant, learned clear, speech on ye Subject: to wch Language & manner peculiarly graced: – he concluded all by saying to the High Steward & Judges whom he called ye Whole Law of this Land, if they thought it ever was or he would acquiesce could be done. "As for me (said he) "I never Saw " such a thing; I never "read of such a thing; I never heard of such a thing, – & I "hope I never shall see such a thing; read, or hear "of it. – What shall ye Laws, shall precedents, permit "the Life, the Goods, ye property – let me say more The "liberty, of a Man to be in the hands of two or three "who may easily combine? – Consider a Moment My Lord. In a word he stopp'd a request that wrong headedness in high & obstinacy continued, & proved ye power of ye of a Law Lord.

16R

〖 73 〗

M.r La Roche was the next & last witness examined — He was to prove that the Duke & Duchess had been entirely misled by D.r Collier — he said that that Man had formed y.e length & breadth of the oaths they Harvey & her took in the Ecclesiastical Court, of w.ch he is a D.r — the Duke had doubts of the validity of the Sentence, but Collier quieted him, repeatedly said they He & Miss Chudleigh were absolved by y.e Laws of God & Man — he gave his sanction to the marriage. what is more extrad.nary he so represented the case to Secker Archbishop of Canterbury that he granted y.e Duke a Licence to marry Miss Chudleigh. All this La Roche most fully & indubitably proved for he accompany'd the Duke in all y.e visits he made Collier, was present at their conversations on y.e subject — heard y.e Dukes scruples; & heard them solved — by this evidence he doubtless cast a favorable shade on y.e Duchesses conduct, She thought herself injured by Harvey we will cast aside her ambitious views in marrying the Duke, tho doubtless they had an influence over her. — A Divorce was resolved on, but how conclude it without proofs of her being criminal? this method was persued & she did certainly thought herself absolved by y.e Laws of Man. as to those of God I fear she looked not so far — but too true it is that Justice is oftener according to y.e will & humour of Men than y.e approbation of God, or to the moral order of the world" which "Shews thee Oh Man what thou oughtest to do." in the words of Micah — to consider therefore the case judicially she certainly had some excuse in what she did. for supposing that she had been regularly divorced from Harvey & marry'd the Duke of K. the Virtuous w.d have blamed her. but y.e Laws could not have condemned her, she thought y.e Sentence as valid as a Divorce. ———

M. La Roche's Evidence in one sense justifyed her; but as to the crime before y.e Court it certainly proved it. — the finding this, the struggle of passion long stifled, every heart breaking consideration arising, worked on y.e Prisoner's mind & occasion'd one of the most shocking fits I ever saw or could conceive. — it stopp'd y.e Court & She was carry'd out — I frankly own that I never was more affected, that very wickedness that prevents most people from feeling for this miserable woman, in my mind added to the horror of her situation — when distress assaults virtue is our only cordial, what a chaos is y.e mind without it, & with the stings of vice added to, every other but grief. — Sensibility is not an inhabitant of her breast. disappointed Ambition; & humiliating guilt are dreadful harpies — it shocked me to see that most of the women Spectators called her an Actress, & were entertained with her situation:- 'tis strange that we are generally y.e hardest on y.e errors of our own Sex — & narrowness of mind w.ch I hope proceeds only from y.e too frequent narrowness of education given many Women, & y.e want of reflexion & the early use of combining causes with effects — by w.ch the evil of those effects may be softened, when we see y.e springs of them; y.e temptations to them; & consider the frailty of human nature. — this is a long digression My heart & Pen are in such Unison that as I really made these reflexions whilst the Lords adjourned to their House to debate on what punishment should be inflicted on her, I give them in this place:— Her fit interrupted La Roche's Evidence on her return

he

17R

[75]

he ended it — then the Lords adjourned to know the proper punish=
ment, should she be found guilty. — on their return she was from
the Bar, & unanimously declared guilty except by the Duke of
Newcastle who said erroneously not intentionally guilty.
on her re-entrance the Lord H. Steward declared to her ye
Lords resolves — She claimed the priviledge of Peerage according
to the Statutes. — He asked ye Attorney General what objection
he had to make to this plea? — Thurloe rose. — He began by
tracing the origin of ye Benefit of Clergy, — the same priviledge
afterwards granted to person of high rank — he gave as allego
various Statutes, acts, &c: by which the priviledge was either
restrained, or enlarged, according to the circumstances of the
times: — ye first origin of the Benefit of Clergy was in
Harry ye 6ths time I think, then enforced by Edward ye 4th,
who enlarged its benefit to all clerical persons of either
Sex — Harry ye 8th at ye time of ye Reformation preserved
the statute in ampler force. — Edward ye 6th likewise enforced
it; — & in his reign Peeresses were allow'd trial by their
Peers, but the priviledge not granted them — & I think
the whole lay in that state till William & Mary
when ye Priviledge of trial was enlarged for Women & ye
Benefit of Clergy rather supposed theirs from than granted
them. — We had a most deep & learned speech on these points
ole ye Statutes urged; much Law display'd; as well as great
Memory. — Mansfield ye Duchesses second Council reply'd
'tho if I recollect right both Wedderburne & Wallace made
short speeches but ye argument fell to Thurloe & Mansfield

17v

Mr Mansfield said it appeared strange to him that the only objection made to Lenity, was that very consideration that should plead in favour of it, the <u>Sex</u> of ye prisoner: a defenceless woman surely might expect to have even ye Laws strain'd in her favor but when such futile reasons were stated against her, she might justly be astonish'd, & ye Court in general; he brought statutes wherein women enjoying ye benefit was supposed — he remarked that in all cases Laws could not be taken verbatim: — indeed his speech was well put together well deliver'd; & had much truth in it. — Thurloe answer'd it briefly, always dwelling on ye <u>Letter of the Law</u>. — he archly asked if Mr Mansfield meant his speech as a Compliment to ye chief part of his audience the Ladies, who adorn'd the Hall; & to whom he wish'd to shew his attachment for ye Sex, & ye power they had over him? if that was his intention he admitted His argum.ts was just, answer'd the purpose. but if he intended to appear & speak as a Lawyer, he was sorry to say he had mistaken his ground:

After these pleadings for & against the Lords went to their house, to debate on ye validity of the Prisoners plea & its admissability; — their first step was to ask ye opinion of ye Judges & they unanimously declar'd that ye Plea should be admitted, the priviledge granted, that as a Peeress she should not be punished as other Felons are with this restriction however that should she ever be guilty of Felony again, it should not be admitted but should be deemed Capital, & be punished without benefit of Clergy. — On their Return the Lord High Steward spoke to her to this effect. —

Madam!

"It has pleased the House to admit your "Plea. but I am charged to acquaint you that shd. "you again be guilty of Felony, the offence will be "deemed Capital. — At present you may be discharg'd "~~without~~ I leave you no other punishment than ye "Stings of your own Conscience — Punishment suffici-"ent for such crimes! — You will be discharged on paying "ye fees. — "

The Wand was broken, by wch ye Commission was dissolved, & all ended. —

—

I have given a long & tedious detail of it. — When I tell you that I have had no help but from memory — I have written it every spare minute as I should take up my knotting shuttle, you will perhaps allow for incoherence. exact I believe it, except where my comprehension did not second my attention — if it is an amusement to my friends I am fully recompensed for ye consciousness of presumption in troubling them with it. ——

Marriage entered by means of an attorney who dictated ye mode of ~~dis~~ forming a register or Check book in which ~~the m~~ other entries were afterwards made — for so inconsiderable was Lainston containing only Mr. Meryll's house that before that time no register had been in being that ~~Book was kept by Mrs Amis till her Husband~~ ~~such cautions were unnecessary~~ Book was kept by Mrs Amis till her Husband Death who at ye time twas made was ill in Bed when he died at Miss Chudleigh's request she gave it to Mr. Meryll after whose death Mr. Bathurst had it who married his

Daughter & finding it a common register Book
deliverd it to ye then Clergyman of ye living

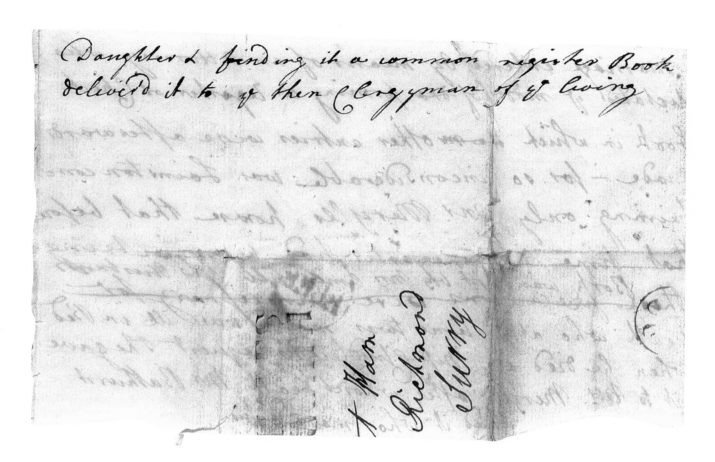

ffor
Richard
Surry

Transcriptions
of Diary *and* Letters

A NOTE ON STYLE:

The following is a transcription of the manuscripts. Where text is missing or difficult to read, I have supplied my best guess in brackets with a question mark. I have silently capitalized words and added an occasional comma or period when it seemed necessary to assist comprehension. Interlinings are indicated by carets. Deletions are indicated by italics. Underlining in the text is retained here. Some abbreviations, such as "wch" for "which" and "ye" for "the," have been expanded to make the transcription more readable.

[1R]
Monday morning 7 O'Clock
April the 15th / 76

I can absolutely settle to nothing.—No Chaos ever equalled my head at present, & I will venture to pronounce the heads of half the People in this great Town. This day the Duchess of Kingston is tried for Bigamy—the whole Town has talked of nothing else, for this week past.—We are particularly fortunate for without any applications, we have an over flow of Tickets: two every day whilst it lasts in the Gallery, belonging to the Board of Works, & this day I go with Lady Bathurst in the Lord High Stewards Box which holds but 36 persons—Miss Atwood goes with her tomorrow.— My Father & Brother go this day with the Board of Work Tickets— & George tomorrow has the supreme felicity of going as one of the Lord H. Steward's 20 Gentlemen Attendants, who go through the whole days [Ceremonies with?] him, & hear the Debates in the House of Lords.—I [have been?] up since 5 O'Clock—attending my Hairdresser 'tho we do [not?] leave this house this half hour. I shall give you a most ample History of the whole as I go through with it every day. Wednesday Morning.— Soon after I ended on Monday the summons to depart arrived.—I was to meet Lady Bathurst at a Coffee House adjoining the House of Lords where she has taken a Room whilst the tryal lasts—here her Company (who had

tickets for her Box) assembled, a Breakfast was prepared &c, but I amused my self in seeing the Peers & Peeresses coming into the Hall from their Carriages, which were mostly elegant ones, & the Horses full harnessd & ornamented.—Every thing was orderly & quiet in Palace Yard, & the Guards were very diligent & drawn up under arms.—which was a pretty sight.—At about ten we all went into the Hall, & took our places in the High Stewards Box, the first Coup d'Œil of the Hall filled with well dressed people was extreamly striking, the Peers were scattered about, & we waited an hour before the Procession came in. You must wait much longer for I'm obliged to end so adieu—

[1v]
Thursday Noon.—You must suppose yourself with me in the Hall. At about eleven on Monday enter'd the procession, in the following order—1st The Lord High Steward's attendants consisting of 20 gentlemen walking two & two; nor was it an unpleasing sight to see a number of these who were pretty, genteel, well dressed young men walking round, stoping opposite the Throne, to which each made his Bow as he passed.—After them came a still handsomer set, Peers eldest Sons, & Peers minors unrobed: these were mostly Lads, some amongst them charming Boys. ^Then came the Clerks of the Council.^ After them came the Masters in Chancery two & two in their Gowns & Bands.—Then the Judges in the same order in their Scarlet robes & Caps.—The Bishops next, whose robes are very ungraceful, & being mostly Old Men I cannot say I was charmed by any of their Lordships—the two Archbishops closed the Spiritual Tribe, walking with their trains borne, & after paying obeisance to the Throne they took their places on the side *of* Benches—the Peers follow'd, commencing with the Junior Baron: the Barons are distinguished by having but two ^rows^ of Ermine on the right arm ^of their robes^ the [Earls?] who followed them have 3—the Dukes 4.—When [all these had?] pass'd the Throne, the [Gentlemen and?] Deputy Gentleman [page torn, text illegible] marshaled them out, according to

their Seniority & so [they?] took their seats, commencing with the Youngest Baron—after the Dukes, came the Duke of Cumberland, who as Prince of the Blood walked alone, with his train borne.—then came 2 ^Heralds^ *pursuivants at Arms* in their dresses of Ceremony, on which are quartered the Arms of England &c—they were follow'd by 4 Sargants ^at Arms^ only distinguished by their Collars, & the maces they carry. Garter King at Arms was next in his strange dress, much like the ^Heralds^ *Pursuivants* only still <u>more</u> on it.—The Usher of the Black Rod Sir Francis Molyneux <u>tres bien poudrée, tres bien habilee</u> marched after him.—the Secretary of the Briefs—& I think the Purse bearer preceded the Lord High Steward, who walked in his Robes, his train borne & only marked by a large black Hat like a Quaker's *& his staff of office a long white wand*—This closed the Procession.—The Attendants & Peers Sons ranged themselves on each side ^the Throne^ under the Canopy, & within the Throne.—the Bishops & Peers took their seats.—The ^Masters in^ Chancery theirs, the Judges.—The Lord H. Steward sat on the Woolpack nearest the Throne.

[2R]

The Clerks of the K's Bench ^& Council^ were already seated at the table—the Heralds.—Garter King at Arms—the Black rod stood behind the Lord H. Steward.—'till the Ceremony began.—The Council for the two sides had taken their places before the procession entered. To give you a clearer idea of the procession & the arrangement, I have drawn a pretty exact 'tho very rough blotted sketch, of Westminster Hall in its present state, & I refer you to <u>that</u>. The dots are *the* meant to shew the manner in which the Procession walked, & the [figure thus is ^the place^ where they stopped to Bow.—

The Procession enter'd—the Peers seated—Silence was proclaimed by the Herald—^[illegible interlining]^ The Clerks of the Council read the Kings Commission to the Lord High Steward, the Cause, & reason of it *& the special enditement to again* Then Garter King at Arms introduced the

Usher of the Black Rod, who with three reverences on his Knee deliver'd the Lord High Steward a long white wand as the badge of his office.—upon which He rose from the woolpack & walk'd to a Seat on the last step of the Throne—The Herald then call'd the Prisoner into the Court—"Elizabeth, calling Yourself Duchess Dowager of Kingston, stand to [page torn, text illegible] & come into the Court"—is the manner he called [page torn, text illegible] Then entered the renowned Duchess within the Bar [page torn, text illegible] by 2 Ladies, handed in by *Mr.* her Bail Mr. La Roche [page torn, text illegible] by her second Bail Lord Mount Stewart.—her ^2^ Chaplains [page torn, text illegible] Dr. Warren besides.—her train borne—her *ap* dress was [suitable?] to the occasion, all Black:— A Black silk negligée on not a large Hoop—Black Crape Ruffles, not a speck of white discerned—her hair dressed, & a long Black hood most becomingly put on.—It came down in a point before to her forehead, & being [wired?] out & falling on her shoulders was exactly the headdress of Mary Queen of Scots in the old Pictures.—Black Gloves & fan.—I have described the outward appearance—dwell on <u>that</u> 'till I can resume the Pen.

Tuesday the 23d.—Now my dear Gertrude I can write without interruption, I will continue my account—I was describing the Dutchesses outward appearance—her aspect was unconcerned, seemingly unaffectedly so—she really looked handsome. The Ladys who attended her were in black & she had three

[2V]

Chambermaids in white very neatly dressed—Thursday she read an answer to her inditement—the Attorney general opened the cause—her Council pleaded the Sentence of the Ecclesiastical Court—the proceedings were tedious & dully delivered. The Court adjourned to the following day—The next day (Tuesday) the Attorney, & Solicitor General, Mr. Dunning & Dr. Harris (Council <u>for</u> the prosecution) were to reply. After the *Lord* Procession entered, & the Lord High

Steward the Lords taken their places, every thing passed as before as to forms, & a most entertaining reply occupy'd us for some time. The Lords adjourned to their house to debate ^on the whole^ on their return the Dutchesses Council desiring *leave* time to reply, the Court adjourned to Fryday—On that day Wallace (her Council) reply'd; Mr. Thurloe drew up the Evidence in a most masterly manner—One witness to prove the marriage was examined—Saturday I did not attend, my [brother and father?] did, Witnesses were examined for the Prosecution [page torn, text illegible]. Monday I attended—Witnesses were examined [for the Prisoner?] every one of whom proved more for the Prosecution [than?] any who appeared against the Duchess; — [page torn, text illegible] her defence;—the Lords debated in their House [upon their?] return each Lord gave his opinion in the following manner. The Lord High Steward seting on the Throne—(Garter King at Arms with the list of the Peerage on one side, the Usher of the Black Rod on the other)—beginning with the minor Baron said, "John *Baron* Lord Sundridge what says your Lordship? Is the Prisoner guilty or not guilty of the Felony whereof she stands indited?" He answered, standing up uncovered—"Guilty upon my honor" laying his hand upon his breast. Thus every Lord delivers his opinion being called upon by name.—The Lord High Steward gave his last, every one pronounced her Guilty excepting the Duke of Newcastle who in consideration of his friendship for the ^late^ Duke said he believed her erroneously, not intentionally guilty. Then the Lord High Steward had the prisoner called to the Bar & told her she was found guilty. She received the Sentence with composure. I suppose she heard her fate before, but she was unable to speak.

[3R]

(2d) She wrote on a scrap of paper that she pleaded the priviledge of peerage, according to the statutes: upon that the Attorney General rose to prove the invalidity of her plea; *he* by quoting divers statutes— her second council *Dr.* (Mansfield)

answerd him, the Lords went to their house to debate. On their return the Lord High Steward on the Throne spoke nearly to this effect—"Madam, the Lords have considered your plea, & admit it; but should you ever be guilty of *the like offence* ^felony again,^ it will be deemed Capital.—At present I discharge ^you^ with no other punishment than the stings of your own Conscience & that is punishment sufficient, on such crimes! You are to be discharged on paying your Fees"—(which by the by they say will be immense)—This sentence most awefully delivered made an impression on every one, the unhappy woman who received it even seemed sensibly touched.— After that Sir F. Molyneux on his knee delivered the rod to the Lord High Steward who on his entrance into the Court ^had^ given it to [page torn, text illegible] proclaimation was made for dissolution [page torn, text illegible] Steward said—"Thus [page torn, text illegible] my commission" & he broke his [page torn, text illegible] & thus ended this trial, of which I here [page torn, text illegible] sketch, but as I was particularly attentive to [the?] whole, *you* I shall draw up an account of the [page torn, text illegible] proceedings, which I will send you, 'tho I make no doubt the Trial will be published, how ever the production of a female Pen may be most pleasing to a Female reader.—

I should have told you that The Duchess had a most horrid fit the last day, which made a sad hub bub in the Hall; I never saw any thing more shocking, she was carry'd out, & the proceeding stopped for half an hour. I must beg you will return my papers of the proceedings for I am so lazy I cannot copy it, & I should wish to have it to help my memory.—Yours Ever,
Anna M. Porter

[3v]

P. S. A month ago I raved about Chapeaux plumied & fine Men, I now am in love with nothing but long wigs, gowns, & bands; as to Mr. Thurloe (the Attorney general) I think or dream of nothing else—A jump from finikin beaux to Grave Lawyers!—I do not [think?] the ^change^ a bad one—I think <u>Madame la Presidente</u> or Madam <u>La Conseilleire</u> will sound <u>tres Jolie</u>.

Do you know Thurloe? He has such a Tongue! & such sensible Eyes! that he may plead any cause even to a Lady.—but I am a mere rattle just now. <u>Adieu</u>.

Oh, I must tell you! Madame Adingdon was in our Box the first day—little taken notice of, & very disagreeable, giving herself a thousand airs. She was not the least acquainted with me, & <u>I</u> did not think it worth my while to be so with her—She was asleep, tired, asked Lady [B?] to go away, who gave her a short answer, to say she [page torn, text illegible] made her look very [page torn, text illegible] good set-downs, & took [page torn, text illegible] was out of patience with the nonsense [page torn, text illegible] made her observations on Mr. Wallace in [page torn, text illegible] manner, to the Speaker with whom [page torn, text illegible] acquainted, he at last as civilly as he [page torn, text illegible] her to hold her tongue for Mrs. Wallace [page torn, text illegible] & <u>he</u> could bear it no longer—Another [page torn, text illegible] that I believe the good Lady wish'd herself away—I wished her so—heartily—Her sister in Law was coming, but fell down & sprained her ancle—Adieu again.

The Husband was there the second day looking as Cross as a Devil & as discontented à l'ordinaire.

Wednesday morning—I was at Noverre's ball last night. Madame Abingdon there & knew me—<u>spoke</u>. —& guess who was there besides. The <u>Sweet Squire</u>—he neither *neither* knew nor spoke to me—at which I was glad—Miss A. said he looked like a Journeyman grocer dressed out for the occasion. Could I after <u>that</u> wish for his conversation—She would not take away the <u>Sweet</u> from him, so called him a <u>Grocery</u> Merchant.

[4R]

A Short Account of the Proceedings on the Trial of the Duchess Dowager of Kingston for Bigamy before the Lord High Steward & her Peers in Westminster Hall—Commenced on the 15th of April, 1776

After the first ceremonials, such as reading the Commision granted to the Lord High Steward &c.—the Prisoner's inditement was read to this effect, that she <u>Elizabeth Chudleigh</u> after marrying Mr. Hervey, marry'd the Duke of Kingston during the Life of her first Husband. When she appear'd, the Lord High Steward in a short speech told her the crime for which she was indited, dwelt on the heinousness of it, on the consequences arising to society from such examples; in a word he open'd the Commision in a solemn, aweful, manner.—She reply'd to her inditement by a short speech, wherein she complain'd of the cruelty of her prosecutors; declared her sense of the justice & equity that would guide her judges; & her hopes of having her innocence appear.—This she deliver'd with composure, & apparent fortitude. Then the Attorney General (Mr. Thurloe) clearly stated the Reasons of the prosecution, adding that a cause of Jactitation was instituted in the Ecclesiastical Court by Miss Chudleigh against Mr. Harvey & a sentence obtained in that Court by which the marriage was not properly annulled but rather deny'd, <u>not admitted</u>; a Cause of Jactitation he explain'd as follows; that on a Man's boasting or publickly declaring that such a Woman is his Wife, she is authorized to commence a suit in Doctor's Commons against him, calling on him to prove her his wife, or retract his claim, then that Court gives sentence according to the proofs. He intimated that the Sentence procur'd by the Prisoner was obtained by Collusion but

[4v]

supposing her Council would notwithstanding insist on its being in force as a prevention of the Trial, he desired it might be read to the Lords.—Lord Mansfield rose & opposed this request, alledging that reading the sentence would lead to farther examinations into the allegations for & against the marriage, that the Evidences given into the Ecclesiastical Court must be produced, in a word besides the loss of time, the whole would be of no use.—Thurloe in his reply maintained, & gain'd his ground.—The several proceedings in the

Ecclesiastical Court were read, as well as the Sentence they had passed (I think) during 3 or 4 different years, & were introductory to the pleadings of the Council on both sides.—Mr. Wallace first Council <u>for</u> the Prisoner open'd the Cause. He began by farther explaining the meaning of a Cause of Jactitation; his aim being to prevent a trial, & to turn the whole on *a* points of Law, whether or not any Court <u>whatsoever</u>, could properly be appeal'd to against a Sentence given in the Ecclesiastical Court; whether whilst that sentence was in force any Court could proceed in examinations; & whether supposing those examinations are made <u>any</u> Court has the power of repealing the Sentence?—Innumerable were the arguments he advanced to prove that these were impossible; unprecedented; Cases were brought in ^to^ shew that they were unprecedented.—To the charge against the sentence of its being procured by Collusion not having grounds for <u>denying</u> it, he indirectly <u>admitted</u> it, stated many cases in which Sentences so obtained had taken place, had been received by other Courts; he dwelt always on the Sentence & its force, avoiding as much as possible entering into a regular discussion of <u>the means</u> by which it was obtained.—Mr. Wallace is universally admired. I give you

[5ʀ]

an account of how things appear'd to me, rather than how they are; I must therefore say that to the Eye of ^mere^ common Sense & observation, he seemed to make the most of a bad cause. His manner is unpleasing, & 'tho his language may be good it seems inelegant from the badness of the delivery, from a heat & vehemence in his manner that rather fatigues than strikes the hearers.—Mr. Mansfield the Prisoner's second Council, took up Mr. Wallaces pleadings when he ended.—A number of new cases which he produced some from Viner's abridgements some from Sir John Strange's reports (which latter had been likewise quoted by Wallace) these innumerable instances rather served to confuse the memory of his audience ^than give light to the Cause.^ The ground Work of his speech was

the same as the preceding Council's, the inferences drawn from it seemed to be different from his rather in <u>words</u> than in <u>matter</u>.—Two Civilians Dr. Calvert & Dr. Winn (both retained <u>for</u> the Prisoner) continued the pleadings in her favour. The Constrast throughout between these was striking, the first joined to a drawling voice a length of periods & a dullness of Composition that operated mostly as opiates on those who attended. The other by a spirited manner, & lively turn of expression rouzed them for a while, 'tho the sameness of the subject rendered his efforts of transient use.—They chiefly spoke in favor of their Court, gave new lights into its forms of proceeding, but both they & Mansfield admitted the Collusion in the Dutchess's obtaining the Sentence.—After keeping the Court very long on these points it adjourned to the following day when the Council for the Prosecution were to reply.

[5v]

I should have mention'd that each Council founded the impossibility of bringing on the trial, on a statute of Henry the 8th by which all sentences given by the Ecclesiastical Court were deemed final & decisive in all cases whatsoever; this was a great road to all the Law of the land; very edifying to those who understood it but you will not be surprized when I say I was not able to retain enough to repeat it intelligibly to you.

Tuesday the 16th was the second day of the Trial.—The Attorney General (Mr. Thurloe) enter'd on the reply. His manner, voice, address, command attention.—His strength of reasoning, justness of argument, propriety of Language, demand applause; & to judge of others by myself highly bespeak partiality.—He began by examining the <u>manner</u> in which the Sentence so vehemently urged had been obtained; then this naturally lead into a general survey of the usual method of giving sentences in that Court.—He concluded from the first, that no sentence or suit of which fraud & deception had been the guides could hold.—From the second he made <u>others</u> conclude the Court he described a very villainous one. In the course of what he said on that head he in the following ludicrous manner gave this account "How are Sentences given? Thus. The Court assembled, the Judges & Doctor's setting round the Table; the one who presides gives an example which the rest follow or perhaps have already given, he falls asleep—maybe grows hungry, or tired, or anything.— 'Come, come (cries he) let's dispatch business; come lets give Sentence!'—Every one is unanimous to dispatch business, to give Sentence, but how depends on the momentary whim or resolve—however (added Thurloe looking round most expressively) Sentence is given & that sentence you my Lords are desired & expected to abide by."

[6R]

(2d) He answer'd very ably the several pleas of of the Prisoner's Council; & prefaced his answers by saying that he should have been asham'd to have appear'd with such pleas in favour of a Client. For by dwelling on a sentence which they indirectly 'tho clearly granted was procured by fraud, refusing to have it examined into, & the Cause tried, either implyed their sense of the guilt of their Client, or their judging the Tribunal before which she was called incapable of deciding.—He threw aside the mere Sentence & highly inveighed against the means by which it was obtained.—He endeavor'd to deduce all his arguments against the Prisoner, from those brought in for her viewed in another light and even turned the cases urged as precedents, &c., into the same Channel.—Their Plea of the Statute of Henry the 8th & the string of Law following it he repaid by opposite statutes, & by Law.—I own here all his abilities could not gloss over the force of that statute, for those he mentioned as contradictory to it required the help of supposition to assist ^one^ in finding them such, & rather must [illegible deletion] be made to mean what he concluded they did mean.—However be cautious of what I say on this subject, for I always remind you that I represent things as they appear'd to my capacity.—What he aim'd at was to bring on the trial.—To sum up the whole, all he advanced was to the point in question, all he remarked was to the purpose of that point.

Mr. Wedderburne as Solicitor General continued the subject on the Crown side.—The text being still the same, variety could not be expected; the wish of procuring it however, exerted the abilities of this able Lawyer.—He ran over what Thurloe had urged; he answered some cases

[6v]

the other had omitted, he gave several to the point which acquired double merit from his manner of stating them; he was still more poignant on the Ecclesiastical Court, & raised many laughs at its expence. Thurloe upon the whole enter'd into a solemn exposition of its errors & villainies; Wedderburne into a ludicrous one.—In one part of his speech he gave a detail of the ease with which Sentences to annull one marriage, & confirm another, or ^to^ do either seperately are obtain'd.—Then he continued nearly to this effect,—"Should your Lordships sanction be given ^to^ these sentences by declaring the impossibility of an appeal from the Court, expeditions to the Fleet will considerably diminish, the Journey thither ^be^ considerably shortened; parties may stop at St. Paul's where they will find the indulgent Doctors kindly ready to accommodate matters according to the directions given them." In another part he said,—"So easily, so expeditiously, so pleasantly are matters carry'd on there, that it has been found on a very moderate computation that a Man who is fond of Poligamy may from the age of 21 to that of 35 have 75 wives.— Now for heavens sake my Lords whatever you do in your private characters, do not encourage Poligamy in your Judicial ones." Nor was he contented with striking at their conduct in similar cases to that before the Court, he endeavour'd to expose it in others ^stating^ the following case was a Coup de main as it hit the opposite Council a severe blow.— "A case was brought into Court (whether of Common Pleas, King's Bench, or Exchequer I do not recollect) as follows. A man had forged a will as if made by a woman who at the time he forged it, he declared Dead in Jamaica. He obtained a Probit of

[7R]

the Will in Doctor's Commons. He took possession of Money she had in the funds in consequence,
for by the will that money was bequeathed to
him.—The heir at Law, or some person concerned
offered to prove the will was false, was forged,
brought a suit in Court by which he litigated it.—
What Evidence did he produce to prove these
assertions? The woman herself whose will it was
supposed to be. She declared that she never had
been dead, never had made a will, was then alive in
Court as they saw. Could any thing be more absurd
than to demurr on such proof?—Could a doubt
arise?—According to the Gentlemen on the other
side the Bar there Could. They say no Sentence
given in that Court can be repealed, they declare it
infallible.—In this instance the Probit was full &
clear, the decision evident. What must we conclude
my Lords? That ^the^ woman was dead to all
intents & purposes? For—She was dead in Law."—
He advanced but little concerning the statute,
throwing his opinion into what Thurloe ^had^ said
on the subject.—He ventured an abuse of Strange's
reports saying they were carelessly, incautiously
compiled. In a word he appeared as able as a man
could ^appear^ after Thurloe. *He* Wedderburne has
not his advantages of voice.—You see him exert
himself whereas the other seems secure by having
reflected on his point, & maintains an uniform
constant superiority which that reflection seems to
inspire.—He endeavours to convince by urging one
to make use of ones own Common sense & shews
what that hints.—Wedderburne's Manner appears
to say I will convince you.—They severally succeed,
'tho the former in the most pleasing manner.—
Perhaps had I heard Wedderburne first I should
have been more struck with his uncommon Powers
& tired attention is a real disadvantage 'tho mine
was very little so.—I never heard more real humour
than he possesses.

[7v]

He makes every one laugh but himself, & seems
surprized that they laugh, whilst the surprize may
be returned that ^he^ can keep up his dry grav-

ity.—Who could enter the lists after these Oratours? Dunning did,—'tho doubtless ill fitted for
it.—To an exceeding bad person is joined the false
conviction of being perfectly handsome. Imagine
the ridiculous composition this forms!—Imagine
that composition appearing at a grave & solemn
Bar!—& thence conclude that imagination cannot
design a more ridiculous object.—A voice nearly
ahstmatic accompany'd with a constant, hollow,
Cough.—At the end of every period comes a
Cough.—At the beginning a hem.—Oh! the
agreeable Oratour.—But let us leave manner, &
dwell on the matter it so ill expressed.—Here I
own myself no judge; a great deal of Law; a great
deal of quibbling on words; a number of Cases
from Chapter this, & page that "as your Lordships
may see"; added to some personal wit on the prisoner; I found [out?] ^&^ there is the quantity. As
for the quality I could not distinguish its worth, my
own ignorance perhaps, occasion'd this mental near
sightedness.—You will wonder at this for Dunning
is esteem'd uncommonly clever.—I answer you by
two proverbs.—"Habit is second nature." Those
who admire him are habituated to his manner &
pass that over.—"Comparaisons are odious." I
compared him to Thurloe & Wedderburne which
would never hold.—Law is not food for every one,
& must be well dress'd & well seasoned to be palatable, a quantity surfeits one at once.—The Person-
ality I complained of in Dunning, was his saying
that if sentences in the Ecclesiastical court were
rendered so infallible, people might marry &
unmarry as they pleased, & even the Earl of Bristol
lay claims to the Lady at the Bar, 'tho he added "'tis
not very likely he should." What use for this sarcasm?

[8R]

(3d) Dunning's harangue was divided into so many
parts, second, third, fourth, & so on,—contained
so many "to concludes" that I thought it never
would end.—I was ready to faint when I saw
another black robed Gentleman rise to continue the
reply; however, I found my disapprobation of Dunning proceeded not from fatigue as Dr. Harris's

want of voice did not prevent my attending to & being pleased with, his speech.—He is a Civilian & has a respectable aspect,—'tho his voice is low, indistinct, unpleasing, yet his manner is good & he has a propriety of action that attaches one's attention.—He began so modestly that I forgot he was the 4th Lawyer who had occupy'd the Court.—He said that after hearing the subject so uncommonly well handled, it was presumption in him to trouble the Court any longer, for he could have nothing to add. That as to Cases it appeared to him unnecessary to cite any to prove what simple common sense ^sufficiently^ proved; therefore, all he should say would be to give them an incite into the forms of his Court, & shew them how far they might proceed in the appeal now before them.—This he did very concisely & well. I left the Hall after this harangue.—The Lords adjourned to their House to debate on the steps to be taken for & against the Sentence.—On their return to the Hall Lord Talbot moved for an adjournment of the Court.—Wallace was asked if he purposed a reply ^on his side^ (he answer'd that he did & desired time to draw it up in. —It was granted him, & notwithstanding an effort was made to conclude it that day, the Court was adjourned untill Friday the 19th.

[8v]

Friday the 19th.—The proceedings began by Mr. Wallaces reply. He had a bad cause; he had sifted every word to be urged for his side before; what could he do? Why no otherwise than he did. Cast away as much as possible the material pointed arguments & dwell on trifles which he twisted about as well as he could; give us case upon case to lead us from the consequential objections. First he carried us on board ship into the West Indies with a Sailor whose wages had been embezzled; then he tripped from turnpike roads to cross Lanes & brought cases from the conduct of Commissioners of Highways, Carts, & Waggons;—he wished to entertain us by his witticisms, what effect they had on others I cannot determine. As for me whilst I was finding out in what the first joke consisted a second came, & then a third like Banquo's race shewn as Kings to

Macbeth. I might say with him, "Another & Another, & Another, & still the last bears semblance to the first—& mark another yet."—You saw a man piqued, vexed; it was impossible to bias one effectually by means of <u>reason</u> against the Cause his antagonists so ably pleaded. He wished therefore by Personal reflexions on the opposite Council to turn us against the <u>Men</u> not the Cause they handled.— He thus answer'd Thurloe's description of the Judges of the Ecclesiastic court & the manner in which they give Sentences—"I have no doubt some time hence to see my learned friend raised by his uncommon abilities to the first Law posts in this Kingdom, then I hope it will never be reproachd him that <u>he</u> left a Cause undecided from indolence; or because his friends expected him at Table; or that for the sake of <u>future</u> repose he submitted to <u>present</u> dispatch of business." Nothing could be harsher than this sarcasm; nothing more ungenerous; for Thurloe is remarkable for his extreme Lazyness & his indolence has been his only fault in business.—I wish it had been his only one in *through* his moral conduct through life.

[9R]

To Dunning who had spoken contemptuously of Viner's abridgements Wallace said—"recollect that most of the wealth he now possesses he owes to Viner.—& most of the Law your Lordships have paid for & do pay for is *fr* out of Viner."—In a word Wallace neither gained himself or his cause credit by his reply.—I think Dr. Calvert continued it; & Thurloe answer'd him by a short speech, but here my attention dropp'd.—I follow'd the example for the moment of some Noble Lords.—I must mention one who when first the Court met rose in a mumble, mumble, & after talking ^half an hour^ for his own edification I suppose (as I am sure nobody else heard him) at last by raising his voice he told us that he moved that the Lords should examine the Sentence ^given^ in the Ecclesiastical Court, & determine whether or not a Trial could be proceeded on.—Imagine how every one stared for what else had they been about since their meeting? However, notwithstanding the general laugh,

& call <u>to order</u> Lord Mansfield rose, & by his able speech made us forget or rather forgive the blundering Lord.—He answer'd & told him that he must either have been remiss in his <u>attendance</u>, <u>attention</u>, or <u>enquiries</u> not to know that that had been their busyness ^for three days.^ He afterwards in the easiest, clearest, manner, ran over the several proceedings for his information; & to help the general recollection of the Court.—After Wallace's speech, Lord Carlisle asked him some very pertinent questions, & the degree of modesty & diffedence with which he put them, added not a little to their merit,—so true it is that the World is ever readier to give praise when not demanded by *b* a confident self sufficiency.—

[9v]

After the reply the Lords adjourned to their own house, to ask the opinion of the Judges, *opinion* & debate on the Justness of bringing on the trial.— We waited for them some time during which I learnt from my brother (who attended in the House) that the Lord High Steward asked the Judges whether they thought the trial according to Law? The Chief Justice De Grey answer'd in the name of his brethren that they were unanimously <u>for</u> the trial.—He said his speech was one of the Noblest pieces of Oratory ever heard. So much Eloquence, so much Law, so much universal learning, such Good Language, & such manners.— After debates the Lords return'd.—The Lord High Steward told the Attorney General to proceed in the Prosecution. Then Thurloe shone in setting forth the Evidence.—He began by awefully enumerating the ill consequences of such crimes to moral order; civil society; & religion—to the Laws of God & Man.—After dwelling some time on those considerations, after enforcing them by forcible similes & Oratorical figures—he shew'd the various circumstances that aggravated this particular commision of the crime, the Collusion that follow'd it, the perjury that accomplished it.—As a stronger shade to this picture he stated all that could be in general urged as excuses to such faults, & then proved that none of these could be alledged

in excuse of this error.—"It was not the heat of intemperate Youth; the force of blind Passion; that led the Parties on—'twas <u>Dry Lucre</u> suggested it & <u>Cold Fraud</u> perpetrated it."—Then again he added,—"Nay it clearer appears that the Lady was perfectly indifferent which Husband remained hers, provided she had the richest, & the one who gave her the highest Rank."—After these general observations he entered into an account of the Evidence he should bring in; which in fact was a history of the renowned Dutchess to the following effect.—

[10R]

(4th) The Lady at the Bar is born of a reputable, of an honourable Gentleman's family; the younger branch of a Baronet's family. She ^was^ educated in the paths of virtue. She was led by the guidance of Prudence & Discretion, too soon she forfeited all pretensions to the precepts these teach.—She was received into the Princess Dowager of Wales's family as her Maid of Honour, & for some time supported the character she bore when first she entered that service.—I am uncertain if Mr. Thurloe said that she was Maid of Honour before or after her marriage with Mr. Harvey.—About August (I think 54 but dates I really forget) she went down into Hampshire on a Visit to a Mr. Meryll's at Lanestown *in Hamps during* with her Aunt Mrs. Hanmore. During her stay there she accompany'd Her Aunt & the Family they were with, to Winchester races. There she became acquainted with Mr. Harvey.—Their acquaintance was soon ripen'd into an intimacy.—The reasons of so speedy a connection we will attribute to advances from the Lady which were perhaps solicited, if not they were readily answered by the Gentleman. Whether he continued in the neighbourhood only, or came immediately to Mr. Meryll's house, I do not recollect but I think the former.—After a short time, a marriage was agreed on by the Parties.—Reasons of Prudence on both sides occasion'd their resolving it should be a Clandestine one. Those on Mr. Harvey's part proceeded from the fear of the Earl of Bristol's disapprobation, & the impossibility of his succeeding in the World without the patronage of such a relation.—Miss Chudleigh's Establishment in life, her being already in the Princesses family, or hoping to be so (points I do not exactly remember) made her readily agree to the privacy of the Marriage.—Mr. Meryll's house was situated in the parish of Laneston. There was no other house in the Parish or rather no house of any consideration.—The Church was at the end of his Garden & a door

[10v]

open'd from thence into the Church Yard.—At Eleven O'Clock at night in the month of August, Mr. Harvey & Miss Chudleigh accompany'd by Mr. Meryll, Mrs. Hanmore, a Mr. ^Montenay^ (?) [illegible deletion] *or some such name*; & Anne Craddock Mrs. Hanmore's Maid ^went to the church where^ Mr. Amis [illegible deletion] the Clergyman of that Parish marry'd them.—I believe the very next day Mr. Harvey left Laneston & went to join the Fleet at *Plymouth* ^Portsmouth^ which ^was^ then under the Command of Sir John Davers,—destined I think for the West Indies. I believe it was two years before he returned, during which time she had a house in Conduit Street where she received him, where several of their friends saw them; & where they lived & were regarded as Man & Wife.—She likewise had one Child there. If I remember right he made a second voyage, & it was not till 58 that a disgust & disagreement arose between them, upon what account the Attorney General intimated <u>only</u>.—However, they determined to part. He sent her several messages to propose a Divorce; offered several methods; at length he wanted her to declare that she was <u>Criminal</u> in her Conduct, in order to forward the proceeding in case he commenced a suit. She sent him an answer of the most indelicate cast declaring she would not.—Upon the Earl of Bristol's being dangerously ill & declared dying (tho he afterwards recover'd) she went Post down to Winchester, to the Clergyman who had marry'd her, & who had a Parish in Winchester, or was retired there. She put up at an Inn opposite to his House.—The particulars of the

visit she made him were minutely related. She desired him to give her a Certificate of her Marriage *& a Copy of the Register* to that purpose *she had brought down with her stampt Paper (a particular Paper used in those cases)*

[11R]

unfortunately the Poor Parson knew not how to use it & would not 'till he had seen Mr. Meryll or some other person who could direct him in the use of it & assure him 'twas lawfull. Mr. Meryll was sent for ^but could not^ set them right, ^in the manner of giving it, however^ she obtained *had Certificate &c* ^a register of her marriage a register book being bought & the^ The Earl of Bristol recover'd; then ^the^ certificate & Register were forgotten; Ld. Bristol's heir sunk into Mr. Harvey & her Husband; she entered afresh into his schemes for dissolving the marriage.—Thus the Attorney General proved what he first advanced that she valued the Husband according to his riches, & the rank he gave her.—She was then as anxious to be Lady Bristol, as she since has shew'd herself to be Duchess of Kingston.—Her first connexion with the Duke of Kingston, the public manner in which she lived with him, are generally known. During that time Harvey justly accused her of Criminality, but whether the want of proofs, or the power of money, or other reasons prevented him, he did not attempt a Divorce 'tho he talked of & wished it.—At length an expedient was found. She was to bring in a suit of Jactitation against him, he was to acquiesce in it, the accommodating Doctors of the Ecclesiastical Court building on the Statute, actuated by the love of power & of gain, drew up a form of Oaths; were dictated in the steps they took; *doctors* formed a Sentence.—In a word Doctered up as pretty a dose of roguery, fraud, & villainy, as ever stood on the records of the most infamous Crew of Civil, Ecclesiastical, or no order of Men.—Soon after this on the sufficiency of this Sentence, Miss Chudleigh Marry'd the D. of Kingston, a credulous, weak Man.—Depending solely on the declaration of the Ecclesiastical Court, whereby she was declared a Spinster.—I have here repeated from

[11v]

mere memory the heads of the Attorney General's speech. You must allow for <u>mere memory</u>. I wish I could have given you his Language; his observations; his similes; he summ'd up this narrative by saying that the Witnesses he had to bring in would <u>prove</u> all he advanced.—That he moreover had the Register of her marriage to produce; *which came to his hands in the following extraordinary manner. The Parish of Laneston after the marriage was united to that of Landcroft Crancroft or some Croft. I do not remember. The Clergyman of this neighbouring Parish officiated at Laneston sometimes. Oftener, the parishoners went to Landcroft (as may be) to Church. There was no person of any consideration in Laneston but Mr. Meryll, the Register book therefore was kept at his House, there being no resident Clergyman & ^'twas^ found inconvenient to have it out of the Parish. Mr. Meryll died, & was succeeded in his House, Estates, &c by a distant relation who of course had the Register book in his hands, 'tho perhaps he had not the <u>reason</u> for having it, that Meryll had, who was in Miss Chudleigh's secret. The register now is in that Gentleman's possession & might be produced.*

The Solicitor General was then directed to examine the Witnesses on the Crown side.—The first who was sworn was Anne Craddock, Mrs. Hanmore's maid the only surviving witness of the *Trial* Marriage.—Her Evidence was very clear.— She was present at the marriage; she was employ'd to keep the other servants away ^from it^; (she heard the Ceremony which was perform'd by ^the light of ^ a taper stuck in Mr. ^Montenay's^ [illegible deletion] Hat. She told us many other particulars; said that the Prisoner

[12R]

(5th) offer'd to carry her to see her Child; that she carry'd her messages between her & Harvey concerning the Divorce. In short many circumstances were repeated proving her thorough knowledge of the fact.—One thing she did not so clearly answer to, whether or not she had any promise of emolument from the Prosecutors if her Evidence accused the prisoner.—It was some time before they got a

flat answer in the negative: indeed the poor woman was so questioned that I wonder she could say any thing, such cross & recross Examination!

It grew so late that there was no possibility of concluding this examination; the Court was adjourned to the next day.

<u>Saturday the 20th</u>

Saturday the 20th I did not attend; but my Brother did. I can therefore repeat from him what passed in order to carry on the Thread of the Tale.—My nonattendance proceeded from my imagining the Evidences would be rather unfit for a Female Ear. —I was disappointed, for I suppose no Trial of such a stamp was carry'd on with the Delicate Decency this was.—

Anne Craddock's examination continu'd ^& ended^ (during which several Lords asked questions, the Duke of Grafton many, & really some his Grace might have omitted if not most.—One was particularly laugh'd at. How many servants there were in Mr. Meryll's family? The poor old woman began & gave us a detail of every Cat & dog in the family; Birth, Parentage, & Education. Lord Effingham <u>talked</u>, we would have pardoned that, but alas! he would be <u>heard</u> too.—The Duke of Richmond finding Superlative pleasure in the sound of his own voice bellow'd out much

[12v]

nonsense.—On Saturday after Anne Craddock,— Mr. Ceasar Hawkins was examined.—His Evidence was clear & pointed but rather a Corroborating than a direct one.—He proved that he had attended the prisoner during her Lying-in, from his connection with, & friendship for, Harvey.—That afterwards he carry'd messages from him to her, concerning a divorce, at that period when Harvey was convinced of her ill conduct but yet wished for an amicable composition.—Hawkins's behaviour was perfectly honourable; his Evidence perfectly satisfactory.—Mrs. Fettyplace (Lord Howe's sister) appeared next, all She declared was that ^She^ had always considered the parties as marry'd; that Miss Chidleigh had told her they were marry'd.—After this follow'd a strange affair. Lord Barrington was sworn to "tell the Truth; the whole Truth; & nothing but the Truth." He solemnly took the Oath.—After he had taken it, he hop'd the Court would not expect him to repeat private Conversations with the Prisoner, for as a Man of honour he did not think he could.—Every body was amaz'd. This should have been said before he was sworn.—The Duchess rose & very generously acquitted him of every consideration, & besought him to forget her as his friend, & regard her merely as she then appear'd before the Court.—He persisted *up* in his first scruple. It was judged a contempt of the Court, & the Lords adjourned to their own house, to debate on the punishment due to such a Contempt.—Lord Camden, Lord Mansfield, spoke to the point, urging that it was a Contempt of their house but at the same time 'twas not in their power to take punishable cognisance of it, as the Offender was a member

[13R]

of the house of Commons & would have the protection of that House.—There were many speeches, many debates, 'till the Lord High Steward rose, & told them that they were mistaken in their conclusion, it was not punishable as a Contempt of a Court of Judicature, but as a Perjury; that private interests were out of the question.—Conscience was concerned.—I believe this set Lord Barrington right. The Lords return'd to the Hall, & he consulted Thurloe who told him he must declare all he knew.—When he had declared 'twas merely corroborating, & proved that she had owned her marriage to Harvey.—The most interesting Witness was the next, Anne Philips. She was the Clergyman's wife who marry'd the Prisoner at Lanestown, & Losing her first Husband she marry'd Phillips the Duke of Kingston's Steward.—She proved Miss Chudleigh's marriage; proved her coming down to Winchester for the Certificate; in a word her Evidence was most satisfactory, & most clear.—I do not recollect hearing of any more Witnesses. The Court adjourned to Monday the 22d.—I attended on that day.—
Monday the 22d.—The Lord High Steward asked

Thurloe if he had any more witnesses to Examine on the Crown side. He said <u>he had not</u>. Upon that the Duchess rose to make her defence. It consisted of 13 sheets of Law Paper—not very Coherent nor very Elegant, but her situation; the <u>tout ensemble</u>; rendered it interesting.—She began by setting forth her Ancestry. Poor Woman. We all sprang from Adam & perhaps she might particularly be stiled one of Eves Daughters if frailty marked the immediate Parentage! She told us the many posts Sir <u>This</u> had *followed with*

[13v]

had honourably filled.—The many virtuous deeds Sir <u>That</u> *perform* perform'd. She told us her last lineal descendant was Sir George Chidleigh, her father's *elder* father.—He was in some battle where he for a considerable time maintained his Post, & defended a Standard 'till at length overcome by numbers he fell; yet resolved never to abandon the English *Ensign* ^George^. He stuck it before him, & the Colours were shot into his Heart.—She inferr'd from the merits of so fair a race that it was natural for her to endeavour to keep up their Virtues in her person; to avoid the shame they would feel were they to think her guilty of such Crimes ^as she was accused of^ supposing they could rise from their Graves & behold their Kinswoman. From her admission into the Princess of Wales's family & continuance therein, she concluded <u>that</u> Princess must have been convinced of the rectitude of her conduct—allowing even that she knew her connection with Harvey, & winked at it. Yet surely she could not have approved her marriage with the Duke of Kingston, which not only had her sanction, but that of their Majesties who by receiving her at Court shew'd that <u>they</u> thought her not so vile. Nay, she said would that great, that worthy, that most virtuous Nobleman the Duke of Kingston have united himself to one marked with such crimes. (Poor Man thought <u>I</u>. Is this the first ^time^ you were called great & worthy excepting under your painted Arms ^in the Inns^ on the road to Pierpoint above the sounding <u>Custos Botolorum</u>). She entreated the Court to consider the interested views that occasioned the prosecution against her, which added she might more justly be termed <u>persecution</u>. It was not the Love of

[14R]

(6th) of virtue; 'twas not the love of Justice; 'twas black revenge; & Avarice.—It was not <u>her</u> they meant to punish.—Her punishment was to be the road to litigating her fortunes.—"Was that all" (added she) most willingly I would resign them, nothing now attaches me to the world, the moment that deprived me of the greatest, best of men, my Loved Lord his Grace of Kingston robbed me of all the good I had in this world, all I implor'd was death, most patiently I waited for it. Had not the duty of self preservation every being owes our Almighty God obliged me to use proper means to preserve mine.—I prize neither Riches nor Titles, any more than that the first mark the confidence my late Lord & Husband placed in me—& the Last is all now remaining, all now left me as a pledge of a Connection, that formed the happiness of my life.—" Oh *Oh* Woman! Woman! How Could you utter such untruths!—Much greater Rhapsodies than these did she spout. She told us that it was the Dukes will enraged her Ennemies, but she said so far ^was she, from having^ had [illegible deletion] any hand in it, he had unknown to her made 3 wills at different Periods, every one more favorable to her. "Encreasing years encreased his good opinion of her."—So little did she instigate his dissensions with Evelyn Meadows, whom he disinherited, that she endeavoured to reconcile them.—That their first quarrel was on Evelyn's leaving the Army ignobly, & the second his not fulfilling his engagements with Miss Bishop.—She brought up that Old Tale which harrow'd up my Soul. Oh I rejoiced at all she said against the vile Man, for of all those on whom the name of <u>Man</u> is prostituted he is doubtless the vilest

[14V]

vilest & so far *from from* ^is^ <u>his</u> mind ^from^ being ^after^ the Image of our Creator's—I am sure the Devil has marked him for his own.—It

was in vain for her to contradict her marriage with Harvey, *that* she admitted it, but said she thought herself absolved from any connection with him, by the Sentence of the Ecclesiastical Court; that Dr. Collier of that Court had directed her & the Duke of Kingston in all they did, that he was present at her marriage with the Duke; assuring them that they ^were^ innocent before God & Man. Dr. Collier's health would not permit him to attend; that she had witnesses to prove he could not attend. The last part of her defence was purposely last. She read the rest but repeated that from memory & shewed her power in the Pathetic, indeed I never saw a better actress.—She ended all, by saying 'twas not for life, for riches, for worldly goods she pleaded; 'twas to beseech them to defend her <u>honour</u>, her <u>innocence</u>. She laid great stress on the words that they might ^be^ convinced she had not made a mistake when she took the sacred names in vain.—Wallace being asked if he had any witnesses to examine <u>for</u> the Prisoner said <u>he had</u>, but previously desired that Mrs. Phillips might be called in to acknowledge her signature & handwriting to ^& in^ a letter. Anne Phillips was accordingly called.—Many Lords rose & said she should not acknowledge her handwriting without the Courts knowing the purport of the letter.—This was over ruled. She was brought in, calmly acknowledged her handwriting, read the letter, said it was hers, & retired. Then the letter was read, all it contained was that she Anne Phillips writ to the Duchess to beg her to interceed

[15R]

with the Duke that her Husband might remain in his Service. She was led to this by hearing that the Duke intended to dismiss him from his Stewardship.—Now in her Evidence, being asked if her husband left the Duke of Kingston from his own choice or the Dukes will, for supposing it the latter malice might have actuated her Evidence, she answer'd so far from it, that her Husband resigned his charge under the Duke of himself.—This letter was brought to charge her with prevarication.— The Attorney General rose.—He declared it a futile charge for it was very possible the husband chose to quit the Duke's service on disagreements & the wife writ this letter unknown to him, hoping to make up matters. Indeed the whole Tenor of the letter proved the case thus.—But as farther prooffs he produced two letters. The first a Copy from one of Phillips's in which he makes a full resignation to the Duke. The second from the Duke in his <u>own</u> handwriting accepting the resignation.—After this one Barton, Lord Bristol's Attorney was call'd in.— He looked so like a Taylor! & made such a snipping Evidence!—He was called in <u>for</u> her, & proved her marriage to Harvey, & his wanting a Divorce; together with all the goings on in the Ecclesiastical ^Court^ more clearly than any witness against her.—Then Mary Pritchard appeared, as arrant a femme d'intrigue as ever lived. God forgive her. I ^am^ sure she was perjured every word she spoke.—She was to prove that Anne Craddock had told her she was to have an Emolument from the Meadows's but it

[15v]

appeared this Woman had been set to worm it out of the old Creature.—Pritchard prevaricated; she first knew a thing, then she forgot it.—She gave no dates, no hints to guess at dates.—Lord Denbigh by very able, pointed questions to her, proved her too evidently perjured.—She said Anne Craddock told her when she had a fortune & could live independent she would come & live with her.—Mr. Thurloe remarked that this was very probable (for Pritchard acknowledged herself the wife of a petty Custom House Officer & that she lived at Mile End) "it is probable continued he that an independent fortune, riches, & affluence, should chuse to fix <i>his</i> ^its^ abode with Mrs. Pritchard at Mile End.—The <u>virtuous</u> wife of a Custom House Porter." In short poor Mrs. Pritchard made a sad figure.—During her Evidence there was a sad Hub-bub. The Witness stood without the Bar with the Prisoner, the Gentleman Usher of the Black Rod, & the Clerk of the Council were between them, the Duke of Richmond accused the Prisoner of speaking to the witness.—The Lord H: Steward

said there was wrong goings on, & charged the Court to be more on their Guard.—I saw all that pass'd & own I did not perceive her speak, the Usher was called out & declared she did not.—My Brother saw the whole & says she did not speak, but <u>fixed</u> the Witness, looking at her most stedfastly & making her signs.—After Pritchard Dr. Warren was sworn to prove that Collier was unable to attend. He declared he could not, without great hazard, but what species of Hazard, whether of Death &c. he would not say.—All the complaint he had was St. Anthony's fire & it plainly appeared that he was asham'd to come in Court, afraid of having his conduct examined, perhaps punished.—

[16R]

(7th) Then arose a violent debate amongst the Lords in the Hall.—Lord Ravensworth began mumbling, & we found out he wanted Dr. Collier examined by interrogatories.— Lord Mansfield answered him briefly, told him it could not be done.—Previous to that indeed the Lord H. Steward declared it an unprecedented thing, he never had known it done. Lord Ravensworth proceeded however, & persisted in <u>moving</u> it over & over again, 'till he <u>moved</u> every body against him. Lord Falconbridge seconded him most <u>vehemently</u>.— Lord Camden answer'd them most <u>calmly</u> & most forcibly.—He ran over the different Laws relative to taking Evidences; the ill consequences of interrogatories; the unprecedentedness of them; the impossibility of them. After the most able, the most Elegant, learn'd, clear, speech on the subject, <i>to</i> which Language & manner peculiarly graced:— he concluded all by saying to the High Steward & Judges whom he called the whole Law of this Land, if they thought it ever was or could be done ^he would acquiesce.^ "As for me (said he) "I never <u>Saw</u> such a thing, I never read of such a thing; I never heard ^of^ such a thing;—& I hope I never shall <u>see</u> such a thing; read, or hear of it.—What shall the Laws, shall precedents, permit the Life, the Goods, the property—let me say more <u>the liberty</u> of a man to be in the hands of two or three who may easily combine?—Consider a Moment

My Lords." In a word he stopp'd a request that <u>wrong headedness</u> instigated & <u>obstinacy</u> contin-ued, & proved the powers of *the* a Law Lord.

[16v]

Mr. La Roche was the next & last Witness exam-ined.—He was to prove that the Duke & Duchess had been entirely misled by Dr. Collier.—He said <u>that Man</u> had formed the length & breadth of the oaths *they* Harvey & her took in the Ecclesiastical Court, of which he is a Dr.—The Duke had doubts of the validity of the Sentence, but Collier quieted him, repeatly said *they* ^He & Miss Chudleigh^ were absolved by the Laws of God & Man.—He gave his sanction to the marriage. What is more extraordinary he so represented the case to Secker Archbishop of Canterbury that he granted the Duke a License to marry Miss Chudleigh. All this La Roche most fully & indubitably proved for he accompany'd the Duke in all the visits he made Collier, was present at their conversations on the subject,—heard the Dukes scruples; & heard them solved.—By this evidence he doubtless cast a favor-able shade on the Duchesses conduct, she thought herself injured by Harvey. We will cast aside her ambitious views in marrying the Duke, 'tho doubt-less they had an influence over her.—A Divorce was resolved on, but how conclude it without proofs of her being criminal? This method was per-sued & she *&* certainly thought herself absolved by the <u>Laws of Man.</u> As to those of God, I fear she looked not so far.—But too true it is that Justice is oftener according to the will & humour of Men than the approbation of God, [illegible deletion] or *to* the moral order of the World "which shews thee Oh Man what thou oughtest to do" in the words of Micah.—To consider therefore the case judicially, she certainly had some excuse in what she did, for supposing [illegible deletion] that she had been ^regularly^ divorced from Harvey & marry'd the Duke of K. the Virtuous would have blamed her. But the Laws could not have condemned her. She thought the Sentence as valid as a Divorce.—

[17ʀ]

Mr. La Roche's Evidence in one sense justified her; but as to the crime before the Court it certainly proved it.—The finding this, the struggle of pas-sion long stifled, every heart breaking consideration arising; worked on the Prisoner's mind & occa-sion'd one of the most shocking Fits I ever saw or could conceive.—It stopp'd the Court & She was carry'd out.—I frankly own that I never was more affected, that very wickedness that prevents most people from feeling for this miserable Woman, in my mind added to the horror of her situation.—When distress assaults, virtue is our only cordial. What a Chaos is the mind without it, & with the stings of vice added to ^every^ other grief.—Sensi-bility is not an inhabitant of her breast, ^but^ dis-appointed Ambition & humiliating guilt are dread-ful harpies.—It shocked me to see that most of the Women Spectators called her an Actress & were entertained with her situation.—'Tis Strange that we are generally the hardest on the errors of our own Sex,—a narrowness of mind which I hope proceeds only from the too frequent narrowness of education given ^many^ women. The want of reflexion & ^of^ an early use of combining causes with effects—by which the evil of those effects may be softened, when we see the springs of them; the Temptations to them; & consider the frailty of human nature.—This is a long digression. My heart & Pen are in such Unison that as I really made these reflexions whilst the Lords adjourned to their House to debate on what punishment should be inflicted on her, I give them in this place.—Her fit interrupted La Roche's Evidence. On her return he

[17v]

he ended it.—Then the Lords adjourned to know the proper punishment, should she be found guilty.—On their return she was from the Bar, & unanimously declared guilty except ^by^ the Duke of Newcastle who said <u>erroneously</u> not <u>intentionally guilty.</u> On her re-entrance the Lord H. Steward declared to her the Lords resolves.—She claimed the priviledge of Peerage according to the

Statutes.—He asked the Attorney General what objection he had to make to this plea?—Thurloe rose.—He began by tracing the origin of the Benefit of Clergy,—the same priviledge afterwards granted to person of high rank.—He gave us all the various statutes, acts, &c. by which the priviledge was either restrained, or enlarged, according to the circumstances of the times.—The first origin of the Benefit of Clergy was in Harry the 6th's time, I think, then enforced by Edward the 4th, who enlarged its benefit to all clerical persons of either Sex.—Harry the 8th at the time of the Reformation preserved the statute in ampler force.—Edward the 6th likewise enforced it; & in his reign Peeresses were allow'd trial by their Peers, but the priviledge not granted them—& I think the whole lay in that state till William & Mary when the Priviledge of Trial was enlarged for Women & the Benefit of Clergy rather supposed <u>theirs</u> *from* than granted them.—We had a most deep & learned speech on these points, all the statutes urged, much Law display'd; as well as great Memory.—Mansfield the Duchesses second Council reply'd 'tho if I recollect right both Wedderburne & Wallace made short speeches. But the argument fell to Thurloe & Mansfield.

[18R]

(8th) Mr. Mansfield said it appeared strange to him that the only objection made to Lenity, was that very consideration that should plead in favour of it, the <u>Sex</u> of the prisoner: a defenceless Woman surely might expect to have even the Laws strain'd in her favor. But when such futile reasons were stated against her, she might justly be astonish'd, & the Court in general. He brought statutes wherein Women enjoying the benefit was supposed.—He remarked that in all cases Laws could not be taken <u>verbatim</u>.—Indeed, his speech was well put together ^&^ well deliver'd; & had much truth in it.—Thurloe answer'd it briefly, always dwelling on the <u>Letter of the Law</u>.—He archly asked if Mr. Mansfield meant his speech as a Compliment to the chief part of his audience, the Ladies, who adorn'd the Hall; & to whom he wish'd to shew his

attachment for the Sex; & the power they had over him & if that was his intention he admitted His argument was just, answer'd the purpose. But if he intended to appear & speak as a Lawyer, he was sorry to say he had mistaken his ground.

After these pleadings for & against the Lords went to their house, to debate on the validity of the Prisoner's plea & its admissability.—Their firsts step was to ask the opinion of the Judges.—They unanimously declar'd that the Plea should be admitted, the priviledge granted, that as a Peeress she should not be punished as other Felons are with this restriction however, that should she ever be guilty

[18V]

of Felony again, it should not be admitted but should be deemed Capital, & be punished without benefit of Clergy.—On their Return the Lord High Steward spoke to her to this effect:—Madam!

"It has pleased the House to admit your Plea, but I am charged to acquaint you that should You again be guilty of Felony, the offence will be deemed Capital. At present, you may be discharg'd *without*. I leave you no other punishment than the Stings of your own Conscience—Punishment sufficient for such crimes! You will be discharged on paying your fees.—"
The wand was broken by which the Commision was dissolved, & all ended.—

I have given a long & tedious detail of it.—When I tell you that I have had no help but from memory—& have written it every spare minute as I should take up my Knitting shuttle, you will perhaps allow for incoherence. Exact I believe it, except where my comprehension did not second my attention.—If it is an amusement to my friends I am fully recompensed for the consciousness of presumption in troubling them with it.—

[19R]

Marriage entered by means of an Attorney who dictated the mode of forming a register or Check book in which *the m* other entries were afterwards made—for so inconsiderable was Lainston containing only Mr. Merylls house that before that time no register had been in being these *precautions were unnecessary for* ^Book was kept by Mrs. Amis till her Husband's^ Death who at the time 'twas made was ill in Bed when he died at Miss Chudleigh's request she gave it to Mr. Meryll after whose death Mr. Bathurst had it who marryed his

[19v]

Daughter & finding it a common Register Book deliver'd it to the then Clergyman of the living.

[and also on this half sheet is part of an address:]
t Ham
Richmond
Surry

EDITORIAL STYLING

James Mooney

DESIGN

Greer Allen

ILLUSTRATION SEPARATIONS

Professional Graphics, Inc.

PRINTING

Thames Printing Company

BINDING

Acme Bookbinding Company